LEADERSHIP

What Every Manager Needs to Know

LEADERSHIP

What Every Manager Needs to Know

Elwood N. Chapman

PERGAMON

SCIENCE RESEARCH ASSOCIATES, INC.
Chicago, Henley-on-Thames, Sydney, Toronto
A Maxwell Pergamon Publishing Company

About the Author

Elwood Chapman, lecturer and business training specialist, is perhaps best known as the author of *Your Attitude Is Showing,* one of the most widely used books in the field of business human relations. Mr. Chapman is an experienced teacher (29 years a professor at Chaffey College and 17 years a lecturer at Claremont Graduate School) and a nationally known consultant in the field of retailing. Over the years, Mr. Chapman has written more than a dozen books, most of them reflecting his lifelong interest in the style and substance of the business world.

Acquisition Editor	Mary Konstant
Development Editor	Molly Gardiner
Designer	Kirk Panikis
Illustrator/Cover Designer	Paul Vaccarello
Compositor	Graphics West

Library of Congress Cataloging-in-Publication Data

Chapman, Elwood N.
   Leadership: what every manager needs to know / Elwood N. Chapman.
     p. cm.
   Rev. ed. of: Put more leadership into your style. ©1984.
   Includes index.
   ISBN 0-574-20920-4: $14.00
   1. Leadership. I. Chapman, Elwood N. Put more leadership into your style. II. Title.
HD57.7.C47 1989   88-29831
658.4'092—dc19   CIP

Portions of this book adapted and reprinted from *Put More Leadership into Your Style* by Elwood N. Chapman. Copyright © 1984, Science Research Associates, Inc. All rights reserved.

Printed in the United States of America.

10 9 8 7 6 5 4 3 2 1

A Leader's Guide (13-3921) may be ordered from Science Research Associates. Inc., 155 N. Wacker Drive, Chicago, Illinois 60606.

Contents

Exercises

Preface

Scholars generally recognize that there is a serious leadership gap in America. Although most noticeable in the political and business arenas, the gap is also recognized in religious, youth, and volunteer organizations. As valuable as it may be, management training alone is not enough to eliminate this failure. What is needed is a wide variety of leadership training programs at all levels.

Leadership is designed to meet the needs of four educational and training areas. It can be used:

• As a special unit within a traditional management course.

Many outstanding management texts do not deal adequately with the subject of leadership. As a result, a growing number of professors are recognizing the need to supplement their favorite management text with a much shorter, less expensive book on leadership. A typical leadership unit can last two to six weeks.*

• As a basic text for a separate leadership course.

Although leadership courses on most campuses do not, as yet, have a high profile, curriculum directors are looking with favor on programs that will close the leadership gap. More and more Business Administration and MBA programs are adding special courses. The same is true with teacher education and social science programs.

• For community workshops, seminars, and leadership retreats.

Continuing Education departments will find *Leadership* appropriate for their purposes. Those already in community leadership roles are attracted to programs that will help them become more effective.

• For individual study.

The format and style (exercises, cases, self-tests) make the book ideal for self-study. These features also make it suitable when classroom time is limited.

---

*A 25-minute film, based on this publication but under the title *Put More Leadership into Your Style,* is available. For more information write Barr Films, 12801 Schabarum, P.O. Box 7878, Irwindale, CA 91706-7878.

Acknowledgments

Portions of *Leadership: What Every Manager Needs to Know* first appeared in 1984 in *Put More Leadership into Your Style.* It was based upon sixty interviews with a wide variety of recognized leaders. Through seminars and workshops using the original text, I have been able to verify, revise, and strengthen the material. Other significant changes have been made as a result of critiques from professors and community leaders who used the book in their programs. I wish to thank all those involved for their contributions.

I would especially like to thank Denis Albright, Dori Briles, and Pam Dowie, all of whom attended the Iowa State Leadership Conference in Dubuque in 1986. Dr. Bill Martin, professor at California Polytechinc State University, also deserves special mention, as do Dr. Herff L. Moore of the University of Central Arkansas and Professor Anne V. Sokol of Spokane Community College.

Elwood N. Chapman

To the Student

Leadership contains three special features:

1. The Leadership Formula (model) presents six fundamentals designed to fit into your present style, no matter what role you play or position you occupy. You can use the model as a guide to your leadership growth; you can discover and strengthen weak areas in your style; and you can use the model to rate others on their leadership skills.

2. The book is full of exercises, tests, and assessment forms that help you weave what you learn into your style as you go. It should be read with a pencil in hand.

3. Each chapter has two cases that you are invited to complete, then compare your response to the author's (found at the back of the book). Ideal for group discussions, the cases are also beneficial when the book is used as a self-study text.

Enjoy your adventure into the fascinating world of leadership!

There go my people. I must find out where
they are going so I can lead them.

Alexandre Ledru-Rollin
1807–1874

The Better You Are at Management, the More Freedom You Have to Lead

Managers are the
maintenance people of
business.

Adrian Chalfant,
corporation president

**Management +
Leadership =
SUCCESS**

To lead. To march at the head of the parade. To win the respect and admiration of followers and peers. To help others reach their personal goals.

If you thought that a leadership role is beyond your reach, think again. It may not be. Why? First of all, your leadership potential is probably greater than you anticipated. And second, there are almost as many leadership opportunities as there are potential leaders. Some may be so close to you, you cannot see them.

Think of this book, then, as a road map that will show you the essence of leadership—and as a guide that will help you organize the skills you already have into a marketable leadership package.

DO YOU HAVE THE RIGHT STUFF?

You need not have a particular combination of personality traits to lead others. No one, including psychologists and management experts, has been able to develop a theory which proves that leadership is merely the result of the right combination of personal characteristics. The experts identify so many acceptable traits—and mixes—that almost anybody can qualify. In other words, you are not automatically disqualified as a potential leader because you feel uncomfortable at large parties or because you prefer reading to handball.

This is not to say that you should not make the most of what you have. You should certainly capitalize on your strengths and the positive personality traits you already possess.

Please take a moment to complete the simple exercise on the next page.

WHERE ARE THE LEADERSHIP OPPORTUNITIES?

Everywhere! There are many more leadership opportunities than you suspect. If you think you are ready, there is probably one waiting for you now.

The Upstairs Leadership Dearth Principle states that the farther one goes up the organizational ladder, the harder it is to find people who qualify for the demanding leadership positions at the top. There may be an abundance of leaders at lower levels, but most fall by the wayside before they get close to the top. Some are promoted beyond their level of competency (the Peter Principle) and climb no further; some lose their motivation to become leaders and opt for pure management roles; and some, those who rise to the top in the business world, often become so valuable that competitive organizations lure them away.

There are also opportunities and critical needs for leaders in other areas—unions, youth organizations, churches, and community volunteer

---

Leadership Characteristics I Respect

From the following list of characteristics (traits or behaviors) write out the five you respect most in a leader. Please feel free to substitute some of your own.

Patience	Charisma
Compassion	Communication skills
Decisiveness	Firmness
Integrity	Fairness
Objectivity	Humor
Positive attitude	Openness
High energy	Consistency
Tact	Ambition
Goal Oriented	Fearlessness

My preferences:

1. _____

2. _____

3. _____

4. _____

5. _____

You may wish to return to this list to make changes after you have completed the book.

---

groups. The leadership crisis you read about is real. And there is no reason why you should not take advantage of it.

MANAGEMENT VERSUS LEADERSHIP

Writers have been trying for years to explain the difference between management and leadership. It is not an easy task, because the two concepts are so closely interwoven.

Management is concerned with achieving organizational objectives. Management means communicating, planning, organizing, controlling, and evaluating. It means resolving conflicts. It means setting goals and moving employees toward them.

Management is keeping people productive, maintaining optimal working conditions, and making the best possible use of all resources.

Management is anticipating problems and solving them before productivity declines. It is holding things together.

All of these tasks, of course, involve some degree of leadership. But leadership is not synonymous with management.

A manager may develop the perfect strategy to make an organization successful, but unless he or she is also a leader, the strategy will fail. Leadership, then, takes a bigger, broader view. Leadership takes you into new territory. As a manager, you may be content to work primarily inside the framework of your organization; as a leader, you become increasingly concerned with the direction the organization is taking. As a manager, you may be satisfied to follow the lead of high-level personnel; as a leader, you prepare yourself to become a member of the group that leads.

Comparing Managers with Leaders

The difference between an excellent leader and a successful manager are subtle and difficult to define. Sometimes a manager is a leader in one or two areas, but not enough to make an impact. Others start by extending themselves (stepping out in front) in one or two areas and then, as their confidence grows, venture further into leadership roles. Most people move from management into leadership positions in a haphazard, uncharted manner.

The exercise that follows is a preliminary comparison. Later, after you have fully analyzed the leadership formula in Chapter 3, you will be in a position to be more insightful in making a comparison of managers and leaders.

If, at this stage, you question the validity of the comparison, place a check in the appropriate square.

Managers	*Leaders*	*Questionable*
Protect their operations	Advance their operations	☐
Accept responsibility	Seek responsibility	☐
Minimize risks	Take calculated risks	☐
Accept speaking opportunities	Generate speaking opportunities	☐
Set reasonable goals	Set "unreasonable" goals	☐
Pacify problem employees	Challenge problem employees	☐
Strive for a comfortable working environment	Strive for an exciting working environment	☐
Use power cautiously	Use power forcefully	☐
Delegate cautiously	Delegate enthusiastically	☐
View workers as employees	View workers as potential followers	☐

In the pursuit of excellence, a manager plays a bigger and bigger leadership role.

Mark and Maria have a lot going for them. He is the new city manager in their community of over 60,000 residents; she is the principal of the local high school. They have an excellent combined income, a lovely home, and both are still under forty years of age.

MANAGEMENT SKILLS: A PREREQUISITE FOR LEADERSHIP

Mark has built his career on a sound educational foundation—an undergraduate major in Business Administration and a masters in Public Administration. He got his management skills early. He knows how to organize, control, delegate, appraise, and set priorities. He is an expert on public finance and data processing. Because Mark has perfected his management skills, he has more time to develop his role as a leader.

Maria became a leader without the benefit of management training. First, she demonstrated her leadership ability by heading several faculty committees; then she was appointed chairwoman of her department. Sensing the direction her career was taking, she returned to graduate school to earn a degree in Educational Administration. She also took a graduate management course with Mark. She now has all the management skills possessed by her husband.

The point is not how or when Mark and Maria got their management training. The important thing is that because they have become efficient managers, they are free to improve their leadership skills. They have the background they need for more demanding leadership roles in the future.

Management training is the best foundation on which to build a successful leadership role. But as important as they are, management skills are not a substitute for leadership skills. It is the blend of the two that provides the winning combination.

As a leader, you still manage but you add a new dimension to your responsibilities. You start to change your image from a maintenance person to a mover and shaker, from a data giver to a data user, from a decision follower to a decision maker, from a manager who deals with employees to one who creates followers. The transition from management to leadership may appear to be subtle, but when it happens, it doesn't take long for others to notice the change.

Grace and Cynthia were owners of a thriving interior design business with seven locations. They were both good managers. One day Grace told Cynthia that she (Grace) had been nominated for president of the national trade association to which they both belonged. Cynthia replied: "Go ahead. Tell them you'd like the job. I'm doing okay as a manager,

ARE YOU READY TO ACCEPT THE LEADERSHIP CHALLENGE?

and that's all I want to be. You are the one who will enjoy being a leader, and you'll be good at it."

Cynthia has learned that some individuals are happier as managers. It is not difficult to find people like Cynthia, capable individuals who at one time aspired to be leaders, but are now satisfied to exercise their management roles.

> *Bank President:* "Many of our successful, irreplaceable managers are just not interested in a more demanding leadership position. It is easier and safer to stay a manager."

> *Utility Executive:* "We've had some outstanding managers who tried to become leaders and washed out. They made the mistake of thinking that leadership is no more than an extension of management."

There is an interesting twist to the entire management-leadership dichotomy:

> **YOU CAN BE AN EXCELLENT MANAGER
> WITHOUT BECOMING A GOOD LEADER,
> BUT YOU CANNOT BE AN EXCELLENT LEADER
> WITHOUT BECOMING A GOOD MANAGER.**

For the most part, the above statement is true. Good management skills provide not only the foundation for good leadership but also (in most cases) the time to lead. You simply cannot become a strong leader until the management side of the operation is running smoothly.

Making the transition from a management position requires commitment. Even for experienced managers, acquiring new leadership skills is not an overnight proposition. Why? One reason is that leadership is really a state of mind. You must want to become a leader before changes can occur. A second, more powerful reason is the "management marshmallow."

Managing a firm, a department, a team, a school, or a government agency always involves a mass of details. There are procedures to follow, reports to write, controls to cross-check. Administrative work is not always exciting, but it is necessary. How else can plans be implemented and productivity measured? Frequently, however, managers permit themselves to become so immersed in managerial functions that they cannot see the leadership "forest" for the management "trees." Administrative work can draw managers deeper and deeper into the management marshmallow—the soft, comfortable, gooey cloud of detail that keeps them from seeing the big picture.

To lead, one must look beyond the familiar pleasures of routine work. Unfortunately, some managers are unable to do so.

The Upward Mobility Leadership Expansion Principle states that those who want to move up must reduce the time spent on administrative matters and *expand* the time devoted to leadership. The theory implies that those who fail to make the transition into leadership fast enough may be passed over. Generally speaking, beginning supervisors should devote the vast majority of their time to management activities. But when they move into the next level of management, the reverse should be true. Leadership ability, not management ability, is the primary criterion for upward mobility.

A corollary to this theory: The sooner an individual demonstrates leadership skills at the bottom of the ladder, the sooner he or she begins to move up; the longer that person waits, the more likely it is that he or she will be left behind in a minor management role.

HOW HANDICAPPED ARE LEADERS WITHOUT MANAGEMENT TRAINING?

Most people move into leadership roles from management positions—but not all. Some make the transition from positions as homemakers, students, and community volunteers. These individuals do not have to fight the management marshmallow problem, but in order to survive, they need to learn management skills as they go along. Learning how to delegate, set priorities, manage time, and so on must be mastered at the same time they are incorporating leadership skills into their style. It is a double responsibility. Here is the way the director of athletics at a large college views the problem: "I'm glad I was a successful coach before I took over this job because I was able to develop most of my leadership skills before I arrived. But I have learned to respect management skills. My transition would have been much easier if I had taken some management courses earlier."

ARE THERE SUCCESSFUL LEADERS WHO ARE WEAK MANAGERS?

Just as we have excellent managers with little leadership ability, we have some leaders who are weak managers. Some are so good at leadership that their lack of management skills is overlooked. This is especially true in nonbusiness environments. It is possible to lead a regiment, run a Girl Scout troop, or coach a Little League team without being a superior manager. The management function in many situations is minimal. Some leaders (politicians, film producers, coaches) may be so good that their poor management skills can be ignored or at least tolerated. There are also cases where the powers that be will provide a good manager to act as a backstop for an exceptional leader. Good leaders are much harder to find than good managers. And managers are paid less.

Still, any leader who is not also a good manager is always vulnerable. Poor organization will undermine the leader's authority and may eventually contribute to his or her collapse. As much as subordinates may value a person's leadership qualities, they still like to work or play in a nonchaotic environment.

It always works both ways.

Successful leaders, without adequate management skills, should protect themselves by enrolling in a management training program; successful managers who wish to become more than administrators should avail themselves of any leadership training available.

One complements the other.

HOW MUCH TIME DO TOP MANAGERS DEVOTE TO LEADERSHIP?

Interviewing top leaders gave me an opportunity to ask them how much time they spend on the two functions. Only two stated firmly that virtually all of their time was devoted to leadership efforts. A few indicated that a majority of their time was spent on what they termed leadership matters, but most said that they devoted far more time to management than leadership.

The most interesting finding, however, was that all wanted to free themselves to spend more time on leadership. One president of a major firm in Boston stated: "I doubt that I spend even half of my time on leadership matters, but it isn't because I don't want to. I find there are always fires for me to put out; usually problems that my managers can't handle. This means I must put on my management hat and continue to wear it until things are squared away. You might interpret this to be a reflection on my lack of management ability, but I believe it is something all corporate heads must deal with."

Ideally, leaders at the very top should spend about 20 percent of their time on management and 80 percent on leadership. Reality, of course, can dictate otherwise. The percentage of time devoted to leadership gradually drops for those in less responsible positions. This should not be interpreted to mean that first-line managers should be satisfied with the limited time they spend on leadership. They should constantly strive for more, keeping in mind that the better they are at management, the more time they have to devote to leadership.

Complete this chapter by doing the important read-and-respond exercise.

Read-and-Respond Exercise

Throughout this book you will be encouraged to compare and analyze the functions and styles of managers and leaders. In the end, you will make your own evaluation and decide just how much leadership to put into your management style (or how much management to put into your leadership style). This exercise is designed to start you thinking in this direction.

In this exercise you are encouraged to read each paragraph, check the appropriate box, and respond with a few words of your own in the spaces provided.

Managers

A manager maintains an efficient operation through the effective use of available resources of all kinds. Tasks include budgeting, preparation of financial statements, creating and maintaining good relationships with people, delegating, appraising results, preparing production quotas and sales plans, analyzing data, setting priorities, planning, and resolving human conflict. Managers control more than they create. Superior in operational matters, successful managers take great pride in quality performance and consistency. Their goal is productivity and profit within their territory.

There is no such thing as a "pure manager." Some degree of leadership is involved in all management roles. Those who come close to being 100 percent managers often operate branch offices away from headquarter operations. Leadership comes from the home office. Some managers shun leadership roles. They prefer the status quo and get their rewards from maintaining a productive, profitable operation. To them, the road to higher management is better management.

Agree　　**Disagree**
□　　　　　□

My Comments: _____

_____

_____

_____

Manager/Leaders

These individuals function first as managers, then as leaders. They feel that good management and all it entails will free them to lead. Management, to many of these people, is a backup or foundation operation, allowing them to achieve improvements (even greater productivity) through innovative leadership. Management is "tending the store" whereas leadership is stepping in front to speed progress. Manager/leaders are satisfied to be managers first and leaders second because it minimizes the risks of being a leader. If they "get burned" trying something new, they can fall back on their management track record. Many have the attitude that good management qualifies them for promotions, but leadership gets them there.

Organizational leaders are more apt to come from marketing, sales, and public relations departments than from production or accounting.

Agree　　**Disagree**

☐　　　　☐

My Comments: _____

_____

_____

_____

Leaders

There is no such thing as a "pure leadership" position. All leaders in all roles must assume *some* management functions. Even if a leader is successful in delegating all management functions to others, delegating *is* management. Two examples: An outstanding coach may be 90 percent leader, but he or she must still deal with eligibility, backup services, and other management problems. A politician may be successful because of his or her leadership qualities, but not all management functions can be turned over to a campaign manager. Most coaches and politicians would benefit from a management course.

Agree　　**Disagree**

☐　　　　☐

My Comments: _____

_____

_____

_____

Leader/Managers

A leader/manager goes as far as possible in delegating management functions to others, as long as efficiency is not sacrificed. Leaders know the value of having a smooth operation behind them. Some of the most successful leaders in all environments "manage" to become 75 percent leaders and 25 percent managers. No small achievement! Sometimes those who move too quickly in their leadership roles have to fall back and pick up the pieces.

Most individuals who move into upper management go through the transition from primarily management roles into primarily leadership roles. How far they go depends upon the type of organization as well as leadership abilities. Most successful CEOs are more leaders than managers. But not all. In the military, officers and platoon sergeants are often excellent examples of leader/managers. Youth leaders (YMCA, Scouting, church groups) also fall into this category.

Agree　　**Disagree**

☐　　　　☐

My Comments: _____

_____

_____

_____

- Management skills constitute the best background for successful leadership; they should never be neglected.

- Management skills, however, do not replace leadership skills.

- You can be an excellent manager without becoming a good leader, but (except in a few cases) you cannot be an excellent leader without becoming a good manager.

- Managers can increase their chances for upward mobility by devoting more time to their leadership skills.

- Successful leaders who are short on management skills can protect their careers with additional management training.

SUMMARY

Case 1: Controversy

Professor Adams is the highly respected dean of the Business School at the state university. He has written three management books. His faculty is considered the most capable and experienced in the Northwest. Two years ago Dr. Adams submitted a request to the curriculum committee to instigate a new course in Leadership for all students on campus. The committee finally approved the request, but Dr. Rosen, dean of instruction, does not feel the course should be taught in the Business School. He argues: "I believe management professors, no matter how capable, are so far into the management forest that they cannot see the leadership trees. I'm not sure they can treat the subject objectively. After all, we need political, community, and religious leaders every bit as much as we need good business leaders. If we offer the course in the Social Science department, we will attract more students from these disciplines. There is, as you know, a great need to train our own student leaders on this campus. I doubt if many of them would enroll in a business course."

Dr. Adams is most upset by this turn of events. His counter-arguments are:

"A good management background is essential to good leadership. They cannot be separated. I believe I have two or three professors who could do an outstanding job of teaching the subject. They already know management and they have been dealing with the subject of leadership in their courses. Professors in the Social Science area, without a management background, would be at a serious disadvantage. Students preparing for nonbusiness leadership roles will benefit immeasurably from the management orientation they will receive. I can guarantee you that we will deal effectively with the subject of leadership in all areas of society. The course would not have, as Dr. Rosen implies, a 100 percent business orientation."

Whom would you support in the controversy? What other arguments would you submit from either side? Why, in your opinion, do many colleges neglect the important subject of leadership? (For the author's reactions, turn to the back of the book.)

Samantha and her husband, Elgin, frequently discuss their careers and their futures over after-dinner coffee. Elgin, an MBA, is a middle manager in a large oil company. Although bored with the job he now holds (because it does not make use of his capabilities), Elgin believes that his training in management theory will eventually spring him into a high-level leadership position with his firm.

Samantha is a successful youth leader. Her national organization frequently asks her to conduct leadership workshops. She feels that she has already mastered much of what there is to know about leadership. She also believes that her leadership experiences constitute the best launching pad into higher positions. At Elgin's suggestion, Samantha is taking her first course in management, at a local college.

"Elgin, I believe I have a real edge on the others in my class who are also seeking administrative positions. I think my record as a successful leader puts me at a definite advantage. As soon as I get a few management techniques under my belt, I'm ready to move. I won't have to learn leadership techniques once I get my first administrative opportunity."

"You'd be better off, Sam, if you had more management expertise before you moved into leadership. Management is the foundation of leadership. You've got the cart before the horse. Right now you are underestimating the importance of management and overestimating what you know about leadership. I suggest you get a degree in management, and then perhaps some of your leadership experience will give you a slight advantage."

"Come off it, Elgin. You have been so brainwashed by your management training that you can't think straight. You talk management, management, management. You never even use the word *leadership*. I'm already a leader, so I will never fall so deeply into the management trap that I'll lose sight of what organizations really need. If you really knew what I'm talking about, you would not be boxed into that position you hate."

Who do you feel has the best background for future success—Elgin, with his excellent management foundation, or Samantha, with her leadership experiences? Defend your position. (The author's views are listed in the back of the book.)

Case 2: Opinion

Self-Test

Mark each statement True or False.

_____ 1. There is no such thing as a "pure leadership" position.

_____ 2. Management skills constitute part of the substance clearly needed to back up a successful leadership style.

_____ 3. Management skills are not a substitute for leadership skills.

_____ 4. Those who aspire to be leaders, but do not have management backgrounds, can learn management techniques along with leadership skills.

_____ 5. You can become an excellent manager and not be a good leader.

_____ 6. You must be in upper management before you can put more leadership in your style.

_____ 7. The Upward Mobility Leadership Expansion Principle says that those seeking to move higher in their organizations should reduce the time spent on administrative matters and expand the time devoted to leadership.

_____ 8. Some successful leaders are poor managers.

_____ 9. Leaders can never get completely away from their management responsibilities.

_____ 10. Leader/managers are more successful than manager/leaders.

Turn to the back of the book to check your answers.

TOTAL CORRECT _____

Is Leadership the Missing Ingredient for Greater Productivity?

There are an enormous number of managers who have retired on the job.

Peter Drucker

**How to Close
Productivity Gaps**

Viewed from a broad and distant perspective, the purpose of both management and leadership training is higher personal and group productivity. Productivity is conceived as higher quality and quantity in tangible goods (e.g., automobiles); more pleasant and efficient customer treatment, resulting in higher sales (e.g., restaurants); and better performance per tax dollar spent in government (library, postal, military service, etc.).

Good management can go a long way in closing productivity gaps in any organization. Assume, for example, that an organization or department is not effectively managed. As a result, the productivity gap is wide, as illustrated below.

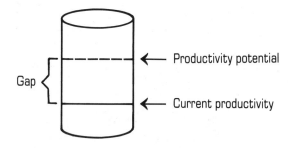

If a new manager (with greater skills) were to take over and were given adequate time, substantial progress could be made toward closing the gap, moving productivity closer to the potential level.

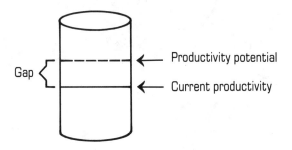

Good management pays off as far as productivity is concerned. But can management alone (all of the best strategies, controls, people techniques, etc.) get as close to the potential level as it is possible to achieve? Or does it also take a high level of leadership?

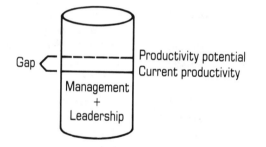

It is the premise of this book that if the Leadership Formula (Chapter 3) is absorbed and followed by an excellent manager, further closing of the productivity gap can be anticipated. Just how much the gap can be closed will depend upon how much leadership is added and how skillfully it is applied. Leaders seem (1) to create changes that lead to higher productivity, (2) to motivate their people from a better perspective, thus gaining more productivity, and (3) to put all facets of the "productive machine" together better, so that greater team work is achieved. Thus leadership training is recommended as an integral (but separate) part of management training.

Although application of the Formula (the body of this work) is the key to supplementing management with leadership, three preliminary factors deserve consideration.

Some managers are unable to motivate their people to reach higher standards of personal productivity because they are enmeshed in the management marshmallow. They are more efficiency and control oriented than goal oriented. They dwell more on cost savings than human motivation. While this is going on, the good manager/leader (following the Leadership Formula) converts employees into followers and gains higher productivity from each individual.

LEADERS ARE STRONG MOTIVATORS

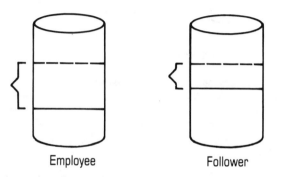

Employee   Follower

The difference between supervising an employee and creating a follower is critical to higher productivity. An employee wants to survive and progress through personal productivity; a follower wants to achieve the same goal as the leader so he or she can share in the victory. Two examples:

Jack is a prototype of the excellent manager. He is steady, efficient, sensitive to the needs of employees, and goal oriented. He involves his people in decision making, provides a comfortable work environment, and gains respect along with productivity. Upper management likes Jack.

Gray is also an excellent manager (much the same as Jack), but he has a different attitude toward goals. He sets goals that are more inspirational and difficult to achieve, and then uses his personality power to the hilt to make progress. Whether they reach the goals is not important; the productivity created in the attempt is the key.

What is the real difference? People *work* for Jack. People *follow* Gray. When you follow a leader, you are apt to be pulled in the direction of his or her goals. The difference is subtle, but it often manifests itself in greater productivity.

LEADERS ARE RISK TAKERS

Many successful managers do not want to stick their necks out, or "rock the boat," because they figure a smooth, consistent operation is more productive over the long stretch. These managers personify the "steady as you go" attitude. Most feel they can "manage" their people into higher productivity through sensitivity and good human relations. And many are successful at doing this. A comparison of the two illustrations below will communicate the difference.

Manager Productivity Chart

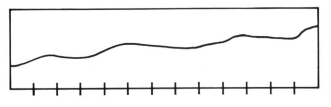

Manager/Leader Productivity Chart

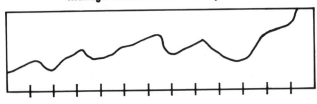

Because the leader takes more risks in his or her operation, the climb may not be steady (leaders initiate changes that are often temporarily disruptive to people) but the long-run productivity gain can be higher. Here's why.

1. Leaders do not wait around, expecting time to solve sticky human relations problems. They gather the facts, assess the situation, then act. Leaders may not make everybody happy, but they are willing to confront the few to motivate the majority.

2. Leaders do not stall until they can make a fail-safe decision. They listen to staff members, tie what they hear to productivity goals, and make a firm decision. If necessary, a "gut" decision will do.

3. Leaders do not burden themselves with small decisions. Rather, they delegate them so they are free to make the big decisions and move on.

LEADERS ASK FOR MORE RESPONSIBILITY

A good manager may be satisfied to wait until his or her superiors delegate more responsibility, based upon a high-performance record. A good leader will see something that needs to be done and ask for the responsibility to do it. Leaders step out in front. They are not intimidated by superiors. They seek new arenas of responsibility so they can demonstrate their leadership and accumulate more followers. Leaders are not concerned about being overworked. They assume a new responsibility, delegate an old one, and move on.

Do leaders create their own "kingdoms"?

In some respects, yes. But not always for their self-esteem or power. Often they seek new responsibility to gain more control over productivity so they can set new records. Leaders are the first to admit that their long-range future depends upon performance. Without higher productivity, a leader can lose upper management support, as well as his or her followers. Either way, the game is soon over.

Throughout this book you will be encouraged to compare the traditional concept of a good manger with that of a good leader/manager. Eventually, you will make up your own mind what the differences are and decide where you want to position yourself.

If you agree that achieving higher productivity from your operation is both a management *and* a leadership function, the formula postulated in Chapter 3 will have special meaning to you. Before you take your first look at the Model, you are invited to review your leadership potential by completing the Leadership Potential exercise.

Leadership Potential Scale

If you have not had the chance to demonstrate your leadership talents, you may have more potential than you think. This scale is designed to help you evaluate how much potential you possess.

Circle the number that best indicates where you fall in the scale. After you have finished, total your scores in the space provided.

	High	**Low**	
I can develop the confidence to lead others.	10 9 8 7 6 5 4 3 2 1		I could never develop enough personal confidence to lead.
I could set a strong authority line and make it stick.	10 9 8 7 6 5 4 3 2 1		I could not become an authority figure in any situation.
It would not bother me to discipline those under my leadership.	10 9 8 7 6 5 4 3 2 1		I would find it impossible to discipline someone under my leadership.
I can become an outstanding public speaker.	10 9 8 7 6 5 4 3 2 1		I could never become effective at group communication.
I am confident that I would make an excellent decision maker.	10 9 8 7 6 5 4 3 2 1		I do not see myself making decisions that affect others.
I can make hard decisions that would cause others to be upset with me.	10 9 8 7 6 5 4 3 2 1		I don't want anything to do with hard decisions.
It would not bother me to stay aloof from followers.	10 9 8 7 6 5 4 3 2 1		I'd rather be one of the gang.
I am highly self-motivated and seek responsibility.	10 9 8 7 6 5 4 3 2 1		I am not self-motivated; I do not seek responsibility.
I have great compassion for others.	10 9 8 7 6 5 4 3 2 1		I have little or no compassion for others.
I can remain 100 percent positive in a negative environment.	10 9 8 7 6 5 4 3 2 1		I have a difficult time remaining positive in a positive environment.

TOTAL _____

If you rated yourself 80 or above, it would appear that you have a very high leadership potential. You have the confidence to be a top-flight leader. If you rated yourself between 60 and 80, you have above-average leadership potential. You will probably do well in many leadership roles. If you scored under 60, you may have underrated yourself or you may simply not be ready for a leadership role at this stage of your life. It is suggested that you complete the scale again after you have finished the book. Keep in mind that the scale is not a scientific instrument; it is nothing more than a self-assessment aid designed to help you measure your potential for development.

SUMMARY

- Both management and leadership skills contribute to closing productivity gaps.

- Leaders are recognized as stronger motivators than managers.

- Managers often pacify their employees whereas leaders inspire theirs by converting them to followers.

- Leaders are risk takers who make tough decisions which, in the long run, usually contribute to higher productivity.

- Leaders ask for more responsibility to better position themselves to reach higher productivity levels.

Case 3: High Producer?

Maureen is an efficient, professional manager. She is a superior planner, always anticipating problems that may appear so she can solve many of them in advance. Maureen has an unusually good balance between the technical and people sides of her department, always staying on top of technical advancements without neglecting her people. She is respected by superiors because of her consistent, steady hand and the fact that she has a "trouble free" operation. When Maureen's boss does his annual evaluation, he usually says to himself: "Wish we could develop more managers with her capabilities."

Gene is recognized as an average manager who often shows flashes of leadership. Sometimes, especially during staff meetings, he comes up with ideas that contribute significantly to the organization. Gene is so goal oriented and sets such a fast pace that employees in other departments talk to each other about how happy they are not to be under his leadership. Management appreciates Gene, but after his annual performance evaluation they often say: "Wish he would settle back a little and relax."

Assuming that Maureen and Gene have identical operations within the same organization, which would you guess achieves greater productivity?

☐   Maureen is the leader in productivity.
☐   Gene achieves higher productivity.

Please state in a few words why you selected one over the other and then compare your reasoning with that of the author (in the back of the book).

_____

_____

_____

Ms. Preston started her career as a teller with a large banking organization twelve years ago. It took her six years to become a branch manager. Today she travels throughout the branch system as an interim manager. Ms. Preston becomes a temporary manager whenever someone resigns or is promoted, until a new manager is trained. This usually takes two weeks.

Shortly after she started this rescue procedure (three years ago), some astounding things happened. Customer complaints would decrease, as would employee absenteeism, and deposits would increase. Management decided that Ms. Preston had a way of pulling a branch together in a short time and training a new manager in such a way that improvements continued. She always left with a party in her honor!

Yesterday the bank management met to fill the newly created position of Director of Human Resources. Although everyone expected the personnel director to be promoted into the position, the chairperson suggested that Ms. Preston be given the job. "She is obviously one of the best leaders around here, she knows the branch operations better than the personnel director, and she achieves productivity quickly."

The director of Branch Operations (on the management team) replied: "I agree with everything you say, but I think her contribution is greater where she is now. I suggest we give her a raise, have her spend even more time training new managers, and have her teach a Leadership Training Seminar here at headquarters on a continuing basis. In this way her productivity contribution will be greater. As a strong leader, she belongs in operations and not in a staff position."

If you were on the board whom would you support? Why? State your case below and compare it to the author's views (in the back of the book).

Case 4: Opportunity

Self-Test

Mark each statement True or False.

_____ 1. The primary goal of management is higher productivity.

_____ 2. In the same situation, a leader/manager can often create higher productivity than a manager.

_____ 3. Most managers ask for more responsibility.

_____ 4. A leader/manager can achieve higher productivity than a manager/leader.

_____ 5. Most managers are risk takers.

_____ 6. Managers are known for their ability to convert employees into followers.

_____ 7. Productivity can fall after a tough "people decision," but increase to a higher level within a short time.

_____ 8. Most leaders are more interested in building organizational kingdoms than increasing productivity.

_____ 9. A high-producing manager is better than a manager/leader who produces less.

_____ 10. There is always a slight gap between what an organization produces and what it is capable of producing.

Turn to the back of the book to check your answers.

TOTAL CORRECT _____

Strategic Model for Leadership Training

A person does not become a leader by virtue of the possession of some combination of traits.

Ralph Stogdill

A Formula for Personal Growth

This chapter introduces you to a prescription, or Formula, for increasing your leadership potential by teaching you how to acquire the common, successful skills, techniques, and principles practiced by men and women who occupy leadership roles in a variety of settings. The formula was not developed merely from reading and observation but was synthesized from the results of interviews with over 60 successful leaders in business, education, sports, religion, youth organizations, politics, and community groups. It has since been revised and strengthened on the advice of professional users, both on and off campus.

In the Leadership Formula ("Strategic Model") as presented in graphic form on the next page, all five points in the star represent a fundamental point upon which leadership can be built. The smaller, inside star ("Positive Force") is the self-igniting spark that extends energy to the outer points. Two legs are embedded into the foundation on which the star stands, and remind us that the franchise to lead comes from followers, not from superiors or organizations.

All foundations or fundamentals are interrelated, interlocked, and interdependent. For example, without effective COMMUNICATIONS from the leader, it would be impossible to create and maintain a motivating MISSION, make DECISIVE DECISIONS, have MUTUALLY REWARDING relationships with followers, and effectively utilize a POWER PACKAGE.

PRELIMINARY QUESTIONS AND ANSWERS

Here are some important questions raised by those who helped to make the Formula, and also by those who have used it with various leaders and would-be leaders. You may have the same concerns.

Question 1: Will the Formula accommodate different management styles?

Yes. The object of the strategic model (Formula) is to put more leadership into your present style, not to change it. A manager who is comfortable with a strong approach can adjust the Formula to fit his or her style. So can an individual who believes in, and practices, participative management. Some people have a strong human relations orientation in their style; others are more task oriented. Some lean more heavily on their personalities than others. It is not necessary to discard one's basic style to adopt the Formula. It will fit into all comfort zones.

Question 2: Will adopting the Formula improve my management style?

Definitely. Any moves you make to strengthen your leadership will also strengthen your management style, provided one is not neglected for the other. The Formula will add substance to most management styles, no matter their stage of development. Through adoption of the Formula, one is in a position to see weak areas in his or her management style not

LEADERSHIP FORMULA (STRATEGIC MODEL)

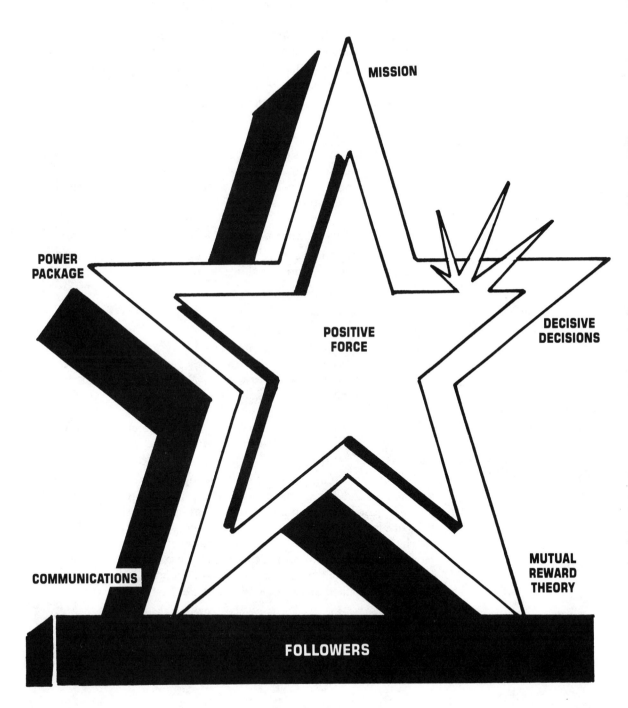

previously noticed. In some cases, a new thrust in leadership development will strengthen the weak area in management.

Question 3:   Are you saying that my career future depends on discovering just the right blend of management and leadership?

If you wish to accept the challenge leadership offers, the answer is yes. Once achieved, it doesn't matter whether you call the results your management or leadership style. Inevitably, it is a combination of both.

Question 4:   Why isn't integrity a part of the Formula?

Integrity, like compassion, tolerance, and fairness, is a personal trait, standard, or characteristic. Although integrity is of ultimate significance on moral grounds, the Leadership Formula does not differentiate. Both Gandhi and Hitler were outstanding leaders.

Question 5:   Will one weak point diminish the strength of the star?

Although one cannot expect to develop equal strength in all directions, a severe weakness in one direction can cause other points to lose their luster.

SYMBOLISM OF THE STAR

Question: 6:   What is the symbolism of the star?

Whatever you wish it to be. Some people feel the star represents a person who excels; others see it as a symbol of authority; still others view leadership in any environment as a "star" role. A few like to interpret it as a visionary symbol that causes followers to follow.

Question 7:   Some authors use a situational approach to leadership. They seem to say that each environment requires a different kind of leader. Are they wrong?

No. Different situations require different approaches, understandings, sensitivities, and styles. The great advantage to the Formula is that it has distilled those basics common to and necessary for success in all situations. It can, therefore, apply as well to a military officer as a politician, a coach or a corporate officer, a minister or a community leader. If a leader moves from one environment to another, certain adjustments to style should be made, but once the formula foundations have been mastered, they can be applied to each new situation.

Question 8:   Will the Formula benefit experienced leaders as well as beginners?

Yes. The difference could be that successful leaders might be content to use the Formula to identify one or more weak areas in their style of leadership, whereas beginners might wish to build their complete style around the formula.

Question 9: Is the Formula designed for business leaders only?

Absolutely no. It will make sense to those who occupy or hope to occupy any leadership role—everything from a student leader in high school to the President of the United States. The Formula does, however, incorporate good management practices.

Question 10: Will the Formula help produce a better kind of leader for the future?

Yes, because all bases are covered; nothing is left to chance. Properly interpreted and employed, the Formula can produce a stronger, more decisive leader and one who is, at the same time, more sensitive to the real needs of followers. This kind of leader is desperately needed at all levels of our society.

Question 11: What kind of followers do leaders desire?

Successful and enduring leaders want their followers to be knowledgeable and fully informed on all aspects of an operation. As a result, they strive for openness and avoid giving any hint of undercover or secret activities. Leaders do whatever is necessary to clarify misunderstandings quickly and promote open, two-way communication. Leaders recognize that their future depends on enlightened followers. They know that distrust quickly destroys their opportunity to lead.

Question 12: Do leaders train leaders beneath them?

LEADERS TRAINING LEADERS

Some leaders, but not all, train key staff members on the fundamentals of leadership. They recognize that the more leaders they have following them, the better. And they seek two special characteristics in these follower-leaders: (1) individuals who will speak up and, when justified, take opposing views; (2) individuals who develop their own leadership style internally but reflect the leader's externally for image purposes. Over conformity that creates blind followership is to be avoided at all costs. As you proceed, keep in mind that the essence of leadership cannot be defined in a sentence or paragraph. Rather, it is to be found in all the principles presented in the book.

The Formula is the message.

SUMMARY

• Most people who want to become successful leaders possess a "trait mix" that makes it possible.

• Career and volunteer leadership opportunities exist in every setting.

- The Leadership Formula is a practical road map, designed to help people at all levels insert one or more leadership foundations into their style.

- The Formula is a composite of successful practices used by leaders in a wide variety of roles.

The foundations (points of the star) are covered chapter by chapter.

Greg and Vicki are enrolled in an evening leadership course offered by the graduate school of the university. Although the course provides credit toward an MBA, students from other disciplines and community leaders are welcome. During the evening break, Greg and Vicki get into a friendly discussion. The are both excited about that night's lecture—on leadership.

"I am convinced," states Greg, "that leadership must be analyzed and understood from a purely situational point of view. Start with the environment and then build a model. The military requires one kind of leader, business another, and other environments still another. The situation dictates the substance as well as the style. I have had nothing but trouble trying to use my military leadership skills in business. I'm having to start from scratch."

"This is hard for me to accept, Greg," replied Vicki. "If what you say is true, then people must wait until they get into a specific environment before building up leadership skills. To me, leadership is leadership. If you learn the essentials in one situation, you can take them with you to another. If you are a general in the army, you can take your leadership capabilities with you into politics. Eisenhower did this. If you are a recognized leader in business, you can take your basic skills with you into government or education. The real basics or substance of leadership are the same in all environments. Only minor adjustments need to be made to fit the situation, and most of those should be in approach and style. Maybe you learned techniques instead of fundamentals in the military, and that is why you are having trouble adjusting them to your new environment."

Whom would you support? Why?

(The author's responses to the case studies are given in the back of the book.)

Case 5: Conflict

Case 6: Potential

Bob Stark, a candidate for assemblyman in the 25th district, was talking with his campaign manager, Joan Burke, about strategy. The discussion turned to leadership.

"Joan, I agree that leadership is the key to any politician's success, but I also believe that leadership evolves in a natural way and that deliberate attempts at improvement might backfire. My present style is working, so I'm reluctant to add any new components. All it needs is a little polishing. Why tinker with success?"

"I totally disagree, Bob. Polishing your style is good, but there may be some fundamentals of leadership that you have yet to incorporate into your style. Adding just one of them could make a major difference to your political future. I believe that most politicians operate far beneath their leadership potential. They have blind spots in their style. And they keep on making the same old mistakes, trusting to image and exposure to keep them in office."

"Well, Joan, if you feel that my leadership skills need sharpening, then I suppose I could study others and adopt what I like into my style. But nobody can distill the basics of leadership. Nobody can say these are the essentials and these are not. Leadership is not an absolute."

"Sorry, Bob, but there must be a few fundamentals that belong in any style. An you may be jeopardizing your political career because of your tunnel vision."

Do you agree with Bob or Joan? Support your view. (The author's view is given in the back of the book.)

Mark each statement True or False.

_____ 1. The essential personality traits required for successful leadership have been isolated.

_____ 2. The Upstairs Leadership Dearth Principle states that the higher you get in an organization, the fewer leadership opportunities there are.

_____ 3. Only business leaders have made contributions to the Leadership Formula in this book.

_____ 4. Until now, most successful leaders have made it on their own.

_____ 5. The foundations in the Leadership Formula are interrelated.

_____ 6. The Formula will accommodate all leadership styles, thus making major personality changes unnecessary.

_____ 7. Communication is not a part of the Leadership Formula.

_____ 8. Religious leaders would find it uncomfortable to weave the Formula into their style.

_____ 9. The Leadership Formula is designed to add substance to style.

_____ 10. The essence of leadership is the formula itself.

Turn to the back of the book to check your answers.

TOTAL CORRECT _____

Be a Star Communicator!

Communication is
something so simple and
difficult that we can never
put it in simple words.

T.S. Mathews

Leaders Outshine Managers as Communicators

As managers move into leadership roles, they go through a transition similar to what baseball players experience when they shift from the Minor to the Major Leagues. In no area is this change more dramatic than in communications.

My interviews with leaders revealed a surprising number who gave high praise to Dale Carnegie and public-speaking teachers for preparing them to lead. In recognition of the need for special training in this area, some Business Administration professors are now suggesting that Business majors consider a minor in Communication Arts.

How do you rate yourself as a communicator?

The Leadership Communication Scale will help you assess your communication skills.

One way to be more objective about your communication skills is to have another person rate you on the same scale, and then compare the two scores. (A duplicate scale is also provided.) The person you select should be concerned about your future and in a position to observe your present communication skills.

Leadership Communication Scale

Circle the number that best indicates where you fall in the scale, and enter the total in the space at the bottom.

	High	**Low**	
I am constantly aware of my communication responsibilities.	10 9 8 7 6 5 4 3 2 1		I need to be reminded over and over about the importance of communication.
I understand fully the importance of nonverbal communication. I always project an outstanding visual image.	10 9 8 7 6 5 4 3 2 1		I constantly need to be reminded that there is such a thing as nonverbal communication. People must accept me the way I am.
I have learned how to keep my audience's attention when I talk to any size group.	10 9 8 7 6 5 4 3 2 1		The moment I start to talk I sense people are taking their minds elsewhere.
Rate me a 10 as a listener. I have developed all the skills and I practice them.	10 9 8 7 6 5 4 3 2 1		Give me a 1. I am a terrible listener.
I know how to adjust my conversation to the vocabulary and interest levels of others.	10 9 8 7 6 5 4 3 2 1		I always seem to be talking to myself.
I use appropriate voice control, diction, and delivery techniques.	10 9 8 7 6 5 4 3 2 1		I've given up on becoming even an average public speaker.
I seem to be able to pick just the right words to convey my message.	10 9 8 7 6 5 4 3 2 1		I'm clumsy with words. I'm always putting my foot in my mouth.
My messages are clear, concise, and well received.	10 9 8 7 6 5 4 3 2 1		If I get any feedback at all, it is bad.
I never over- or undertalk; I'm always on target.	10 9 8 7 6 5 4 3 2 1		I either say too much or too little.
I instinctively know which media to use, and I fully employ all communication systems available.	10 9 8 7 6 5 4 3 2 1		Not only do I fail to use the right media, I do not take advantage of the opportunities available.

TOTAL _____

If you rated yourself 80 or above, you appear to possess outstanding communication skills. If you rated yourself between 60 and 80, you may be getting a signal that some improvement is necessary if you are to reach your leadership potential. If you rated yourself under 60, it would appear that substantial improvement is necessary.

Leadership Communication Scale

Circle the number that best indicates where you fall in the scale, and enter the total in the space at the bottom.

	High	**Low**	
I am constantly aware of my communication responsibilities.	10 9 8 7 6 5 4 3 2 1		I need to be reminded over and over about the importance of communication.
I understand fully the importance of nonverbal communication. I always project an outstanding visual image.	10 9 8 7 6 5 4 3 2 1		I constantly need to be reminded that there is such a thing as nonverbal communication. People must accept me the way I am.
I have learned how to keep my audience's attention when I talk to any size group.	10 9 8 7 6 5 4 3 2 1		The moment I start to talk I sense people are taking their minds elsewhere.
Rate me a 10 as a listener. I have developed all the skills and I practice them.	10 9 8 7 6 5 4 3 2 1		Give me a 1. I am a terrible listener.
I know how to adjust my conversation to the vocabulary and interest levels of others.	10 9 8 7 6 5 4 3 2 1		I always seem to be talking to myself.
I use appropriate voice control, diction, and delivery techniques.	10 9 8 7 6 5 4 3 2 1		I've given up on becoming even an average public speaker.
I seem to be able to pick just the right words to convey my message.	10 9 8 7 6 5 4 3 2 1		I'm clumsy with words. I'm always putting my foot in my mouth.
My messages are clear, concise, and very well received.	10 9 8 7 6 5 4 3 2 1		If I get any feedback at all, it is bad.
I never over- or undertalk; I'm always on target.	10 9 8 7 6 5 4 3 2 1		I either say too much or too little.
I instinctively know which media to use, and I fully employ all communication systems available.	10 9 8 7 6 5 4 3 2 1		Not only do I fail to use the right media, I do not take advantage of the opportunities available.

TOTAL _____

If you rated yourself 80 or above, you appear to possess outstanding communication skills. If you rated yourself between 60 and 80, you may be getting a signal that some improvement is necessary if you are to reach your leadership potential. If you rated yourself under 60, it would appear that substantial improvement is necessary.

As the leadership rating scale demonstrates, communication is much more than being an excellent speaker. Like a baseball player, a successful leader must learn to cover all four bases in playing the communications game. The remainder of this chapter will follow the baseball outline.

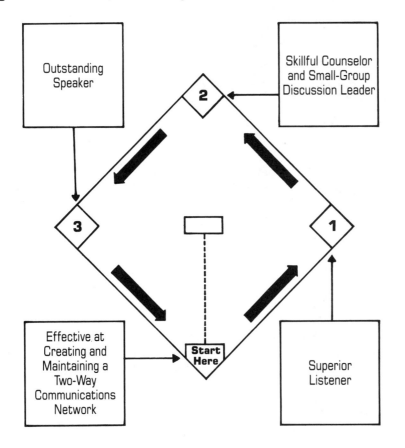

Followers have little radar sets—so to speak—that are constantly tuned into their leaders. Followers know when they are being listened to and when they are being tuned out. When they no longer believe their leader hears them, they start looking for a new one.

FIRST BASE: LEADERS MUST BECOME SUPERIOR LISTENERS

Conversations with followers will usually bring comments similar to these:

"I don't think my leader is as good at listening as she thinks she is."

"I have, when possible, walked away from leaders who failed to consult me."

"Leaders unseat themselves when they make the mistake of listening to a few close followers and ignoring the rest of us."

Ask Yourself These Questions

	Yes	No
Do I listen as well as I speak?	☐	☐
Do I allow subordinates to express their thoughts without interruptions?	☐	☐
Do I know what my followers (or friends) are really thinking?	☐	☐
Do I have a reputation among my colleagues as a good listener?	☐	☐

In your quest to become a better leader, write in the box below the percentage improvement you would like to achieve in your listening skills.

%

SECOND BASE: LEADERS MUST BE EXPERTS AT ONE-ON-ONE COMMUNICATION

Good leaders know when to be quiet listeners. They also know when to be engaging conversationalists. They know how to start informal, one-on-one conversations in any environment. They are experts at dissipating psychological barriers between themselves and their followers. They are perceptive in the questions they ask; they are skilled in the way they ask them.

In only a few moments, a good leader can introduce an important subject, communicate a goal, and reinforce a relationship with a subordinate who may have been neglected or who may have been headed in the wrong direction. A good leader has a way of gaining attention, conveying a message, and leaving a subordinate with the sense that he or she had been a full partner in the dialogue. When successful leaders circulate, they leave a wake of newly challenged followers behind them.

When successful leaders counsel their subordinates, they practice the 5 R's of communication.

RIGHT PURPOSE: They counsel only when there is high probability it will improve the leader-follower relationship.

RIGHT TIMING: They counsel only when the mood on both sides appears appropriate.

RIGHT PLACE:	They select private locations where there will be few interruptions and the subordinate's privacy is protected.
RIGHT APPROACH:	They are nonthreatening in their approach.
RIGHT TECHNIQUE:	When it is necessary to discipline followers, they also inspire them to improve.

Ask Yourself These Questions

	Yes	No
Do people enjoy private conversations with you to the point that they seek you out?	☐	☐
Can you quickly establish a nonthreatening conversational climate with a subordinate?	☐	☐
Can you give followers the impression they have done 50 percent of the talking even if they have not?	☐	☐
Can you, through a private conversation, convert a disenchanted employee into a disciple?	☐	☐

Write the percentage of improvement you would like to see in your one-on-one communications.

%

Dr. Lockwood's colleagues could not figure why her students were so enthusiastic about her seminars at the university. Was it her youth and style? Her command of her subject? If asked, Dr. Lockwood's students would have talked about her touch in working with small groups—her ability to draw a reluctant student into a discussion, her skill at turning a hostile student's response into a statement the group could deal with positively, her competency at sensing and articulating the meaning and mood of group discussions. Most of all, they would have mentioned how she used just the right amount of leadership to keep the group on track without stifling creativity.

A leader must be tuned into the dynamics of small groups. He or she must know how to facilitate consensus and at the same time improve

LEADERS MUST BE STUDENTS OF SMALL-GROUP DYNAMICS

relationships with all those involved. This is not an easy task. Still, a leader who cannot function well in a small-group setting is severely handicapped.

Ask Yourself These Questions

	Yes	No
Are you relaxed, comfortable, and effective when leading a small-group discussion?	☐	☐
Can you perceive and communicate group thinking patterns back to the members, so that the best decision is made?	☐	☐
Can you redirect a complacent group in the right direction, without discouraging contributions from one or more members?	☐	☐

What percentage of improvement would you like to see in your small-group communication skills?

_____ %

SMALL-GROUP COMMUNICATION

Very critical to a leader's success is staff selection. Many people have lost their opportunities to lead because they failed to surround themselves with the best advisors. Some experts give staff selection top priority. But it is not only selection, it is also the development of good relationships through group communication. If you conduct staff meetings or anticipate doing so, please answer the staff-meeting questions on the next page.

Successful leaders have the capacity to develop an inner circle of staff people who are loyal and competent. A good leader's staff becomes an

---

Staff Meetings

	Yes	No
Does everyone have the opportunity to speak openly on all issues?	☐	☐
Do you create an *esprit de corps*—a spirit that encourages loyalty and avoids dissension?	☐	☐
Do you sense, after most staff meetings, that vertical relationships between you and each member (and horizontal relationships among staff members) have improved?	☐	☐

What percentage of improvement would you like to achieve?

| % |

---

extension of his or her image or leadership style. Good communication skills help to create, and maintain, the close bond between a leader and his or her staff.

All highly successful leaders—coaches, ministers, community leaders, corporate executives, and politicians—eventually become small-group communication experts. Many take special seminars early in their development to enhance these skills.

All leaders take advantage of opportunities to speak to large groups. Some are inspirational, and their leadership image is greatly enhanced; some are moderately inspirational, and their image is protected. Those who are credible (but noninspirational) speakers need to compensate by improving their image in other areas.

When it comes to leadership, becoming an outstanding speaker is a *major* advantage.

THIRD BASE:
LEADERS BECOME
SUPERIOR SPEAKERS

Ask Yourself These Questions

	Yes	No
Do you have enough confidence to speak to large audiences?	☐	☐
Are you good at audience analysis?	☐	☐
Are you skilllful at receiving, interpreting, and answering difficult questions in large groups?	☐	☐
After speaking to a large group, do you feel good about yourself and your speaking skills?	☐	☐

Write the percentage improvement you would like to see in your large-group speaking skills.

%

WRITING SKILLS SHOULD NOT BE NEGLECTED

Few leaders are in a position to employ professional ghost writers (although some may hide behind the skills of a gifted secretary or assistant). Most must rely on their own competencies. They must—word by word, sentence by sentence—write their own letters, bulletins, and memos to people outside and inside the organization. They must make sure their written messages will grab the reader's attention, carry the message they wish to convey, not be misinterpreted, and be free from errors.

Subordinates want their leader's messages to reflect his or her leadership style. They want powerful and decisive messages. Otherwise, the absence of the leader's stamp is quickly noted.

HOME BASE: CREATE AND MAINTAIN A COMMUNICATIONS NETWORK

Two-way information and communication networks are more critical to leaders than to managers because leaders are more vulnerable to disenchanted followers and competitive factions. Thus, to protect themselves, they need advance information on problem situations that only a good communication system can provide.

Just as a baseball team employs talent scouts, leaders need people they can trust to keep them informed about all phases of their operation. In an efficient network, this data can come from three primary sources:

Inside Follower Contacts. No matter how large the organization, a leader needs feedback from followers at all levels, especially those at the

---

Ask Yourself These Questions

	Yes	No
Are you proud of your writing skills?	☐	☐
Do your writing skills command as much attention and response as your verbal skills?	☐	☐
Do you use the telephone to avoid writing messages, even when the printed form is more effective?	☐	☐
Do you depend too much on the writing skills of others to protect your leadership image?	☐	☐

Write the percentage of improvement you would like to show in your written communications.

%

---

bottom of the hierarchy. This may mean frequent visits and informal interviews with various departments or branches. One-on-one counseling can be a gold mine for finding out how followers really feel.

Outside Professional Contacts.   Most leaders are not satisfied to depend exclusively on inside contacts. They know that outsiders have knowledge about an organization insiders are not privy to. Also, outsiders view things differently than insiders. That is why professional consultants often play a key role.

Staff Information Magnets.   Some staff members are better as reliable information providers than others. These individuals should be encouraged, protected, and complimented. At the same time, favoritism should not be shown. Also, a leader should guard against overdependence on one source and the possibility that jealousies might be generated.

Although one goal of a communication system is to identify problems ahead of time so that solutions can be reached before a major conflict arises, a much larger goal is a steady flow of accurate data for decision making.

For leaders to be star communicators ("Major Leaguers"), they must learn to cover all four "bases." They must be alert listeners, sensitive counselors and staff leaders, excellent speakers, and—to get to home plate and score—they must devise a networking system to fit their organization and their personality.

The easiest way to lose a franchise to lead is to neglect followers.

SUMMARY

- To become a successful leader, one must excel at listening, counseling, and other forms of communication.

- Leaders must be superior listeners to know what followers are thinking.

- Understanding the dynamics of a small group facilitates productive staff meetings.

- Through sensitive one-on-one conversations, leaders can convert reluctant followers into disciples.

- Leaders greatly enhance their image when they become stars at public speaking.

- To keep informed for decision making, leaders need an efficient, two-way networking system.

- Failure to become superior communicators leaves many managers behind in the leadership race.

Bettina Blake has, for some time, been debating in her mind whether to strengthen her communications skills by taking a course in public speaking. She has been told by close friends that although she has natural ability as a speaker, she should take a course to sharpen her skills. But every time a course is offered, Bettina backs away from making a decision. She rationalizes that she can become better without formal help.

Yesterday she was invited to speak to over five hundred people at a convention next spring. She accepted, knowing it would be her biggest, most important audience ever. The talk will be critical to her leadership image. In making her plans, she figures she has three possibilities for improving her speaking skills:

1. Use video tape to improve her speaking ability on a do-it-yourself basis.

2. Take a course in public speaking. Ample time remains.

3. Rely on her natural ability, but get more experience in front of groups of all sizes before the big day arrives.

Which of the above strategies do you feel would provide Ms. Blake with the most help? Second? Third? If you were in her shoes, what additional experiences would you seek? (The author's rankings are given in the back of the book.)

Case 7: Improvement

Case 8:
Enhancement

Regina and Matthew, both in their mid-thirties, have attained middle-management positions with a large utility. Although there has been considerable downsizing in the firm recently, both feel secure in their positions and can see opportunities for further growth.

Yesterday, after working later than usual, Regina and Matthew decided to let the heavy downtown traffic dissipate before returning home, and their conversation turned in the direction of career progress.

"Regina," said Matthew, "so far our progress has been similar, but from now on I think it is a new ball game. Our progress will depend as much on our leadership as on our management ability."

"I agree," replied Regina. "That is why I have decided to go back to the university and get a master's degree in Communication Arts. I think it is the best way to put more leadership into my management style. What do you think?"

"I think it would be a mistake. What you really need is a master's in Business Administration. At least that is going to be *my* ticket."

"MBAs are a dime a dozen around here. Becoming a superior platform speaker and all-around communicator will enhance my leadership ability better than more management training. You want an MBA for status purposes more than for what it will do for your capacity to lead."

Would you defend Regina or Matthew?

Earning an MBA will contribute to Matthew's management and leadership ability. It is his best bet.   ☐

Regina has the right idea. Communication training will do more for her leadership skill than a higher degree in management. (The author's comments are given in the back of the book.)   ☐

Mark each statement True or False.

_____ 1. To demonstrate leadership, managers must be measurably better at all phases of communication than their followers.

_____ 2. For both leaders and managers, nonverbal communication is more important than verbal.

_____ 3. Would-be leaders should start delegating writing responsibilities while they are managers.

_____ 4. Followers want to be inspired by their leaders; platform speaking provides the best way for leaders to do this.

_____ 5. Communication is part of the glue that holds the Leadership Formula (star) together.

_____ 6. A person who scores below 60 on the Leadership Communication Scale could never be a leader.

_____ 7. Leaders who are poor listeners often lose their followers without knowing why.

_____ 8. The 5 R's refer to public-speaking techniques.

_____ 9. Staff members should be an extension of the leader's leadership style.

_____ 10. The foundation of the Leadership Formula is followers.

Turn to the back of the book to check your answers.

TOTAL CORRECT _____

Convert Employees into Followers

Leadership is a process of
mutual stimulation which,
by the interplay of individual
differences, controls human
energy in the pursuit of a
common goal.

P. Pigors

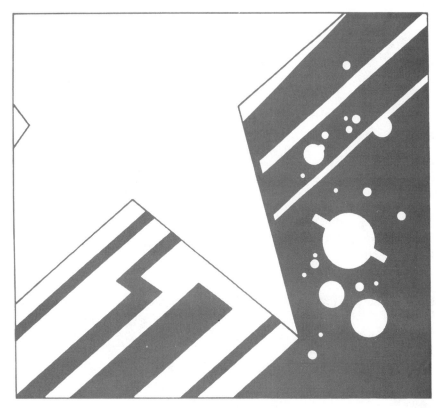

Leaders Provide Special Rewards to Followers

It stands to reason that a leader cannot be a leader without followers. But what is a follower? Is a follower really different from an employee? If so, how can a manager convert employees to followers and become a leader?

The line that separates an employee from a follower is a fine one, and three factors are involved in the transition.

1. Employees cannot be forced or cajoled into becoming followers. It is purely voluntary on their part. If they want to move in the direction the leader has chosen, they join up. Naturally, they reason it is to their advantage to do so.

2. The vision projected by the leader is a primary persuader. The goal or mission must offer the promise of taking employees away from work as work and raise expectations to such a level that following is considered natural and enjoyable.

3. The personality of the leader plays a significant role in the conversion. Sometimes charisma is present; sometimes it is not. There must, however, be a degree of trust and a strong belief that life will become better as a follower than as an employee.

All leaders go about converting employees to followers in the leader's individual style.

When Mrs. Grace took over the computerized office, no employee would have opted to follow the person she replaced. Six months later, when Mrs. Grace was promoted within the company, almost every employee wanted to follow her to her new assignment. During the interim, Mrs. Grace had created an exciting working environment, made each employee feel like a team member, raised levels of expectations, and shared both small and large victories in staff meetings and informal gatherings. As one individual stated during a departure party: "It's hard to put your finger on it, but I felt better about myself under her leadership. My pay and benefits didn't change, but my attitude toward work and productivity certainly did. She provided rewards that are intangible."

HOW MANAGERS OFTEN VIEW EMPLOYEES

Managers are apt to view those under their supervision as owing them (or the company) productivity in return for pay and benefits. It is a contractual exchange system. The company attempts to provide a good working environment, fair treatment according to the laws, and as many psychological rewards as possible. In return, the employee produces according to accepted norms. Those who seek promotions (or are motivated by other reasons) produce more. Even under managers with good human relations skills, you hear such phrases as "Another day at the office" and "Another day, another dollar." Somehow, most employees feel "managed" and uninspired during their working hours.

Leaders train themselves to view employees as people who will become followers, providing they are given a taste of victory. With this perspective, the leader is acknowledging that employees want to be led out of the typical work malaise. *They want to be led, not managed*—providing, of course, the demands on being a follower are within reason. Employees do not want work to be *work*. It is not that they do not want to produce; they want a leader who will inspire them above and beyond the mundane tasks that constitute productivity. For those who can do this, they are usually willing to produce at higher levels.

Just as employees respond differently to their manager, they also respond differently to the leader. Thus a leader cannot expect to convert all employees into enthusiastic followers. Followers, nevertheless, seem to pull others along with them.

HOW LEADERS VIEW EMPLOYEES

How Employees View Managers vs. Leaders

This exercise is designed to help you perceive how some employees view managers and how some followers view their leaders. If any of the views come close to fitting your environment (as an employee, manager, or leader), please check the appropriate box.

Many employees view managers as superiors who are paid to control an operation, not lead it. Here are three typical employee attitudes.

☐ "I feel somewhat restricted and 'pegged' in my job. To satisfy my manager, all I need do is live up to my job description. It is all so mechanical. Despite all the coworkers that surround me, I often feel isolated. I need to sense I am going somewhere. I have lost my ability to lift myself up, and my manager does not seem to be concerned."

☐ "My manager often talks about a team effort, but little seems to happen to facilitate it. I work harder than others because I seek a promotion and a way out of my present condition. I am on friendly terms with my fellow workers, but I do not have a 'team' feeling. I think my manager is trying to do all the right things. She is as efficient, sensitive, and supportive as one could expect. It is just that there is so little to anticipate."

☐ "We have an outstanding manager, but frankly I still feel I am not accomplishing anything or really enjoying my job. I think it boils down to a matter of pride. I would like to feel I am part of a team that is winning a race that is important. I would like to break loose and contribute to something bigger so that everyone could share. I would like to brag to my family about what is happening to me on the job."

An employee who works under a leader and becomes a follower often has a different view:

☐ "When I worked under a manager, I felt like all of us were trying to hold a big rock up more than we were trying to push it in any direction. Now that I work for a leader, it is like we are all trying to push the rock over a cliff, and when it happens we will all celebrate. I have never been a good team member, but I'm enjoying work more and producing at a higher level."

☐ "Since my transfer, I find myself volunteering more. I am looking for ways to improve the operation even though I do not get credit. I believe the difference lies in having a leader instead of a manager. We have fun, we violate a few minor rules, but we also produce. I feel rewarded as a team member. It is not just a compliment now and then; it's a feeling of pride that we all share."

☐ "Frankly, if Mr. Harris were to be transferred I would like to go with him. He generates so much excitement around here that those in other departments are envious. He seems to know what kinds of rewards make life better for us. It's not that other managers are not accessible, capable, and good to their people; it is just that Mr. Harris seems to be free of the management chains that keep others from being leaders. Of course, a few members of our department would prefer to slide back into their old comfortable ways. Not me."

Regardless of which blocks you did or did not check, exploring the strategies or techniques leaders use to convert employees into followers is exciting. Although many factors are involved, the primary way to convert employees into followers is to practice the Mutual Reward Theory.

If you have ever observed two monkeys grooming each other you have seen the Mutual Reward Theory (MRT) operating as its most basic level. When MRT works, both parties come out ahead. In the case of the monkeys, they both have something done for them that they cannot do effectively by themselves. Their lives are thereby enhanced.

MUTUAL REWARD THEORY

Your first reaction may be that MRT is no more than a truism, just another restatement of the old human relations principle: "If you scratch my back, I'll scratch yours."

When it comes to leadership, it is much more.

MRT states that a relationship between two people (or groups) is improved and enhanced when there is a satisfactory exchange of rewards between them. It is upon this human relations principle that all leader-follower relationships are built. Unless both parties (leader and follower) come out ahead, the relationship will not last. MRT is, therefore, one of the irreplaceable foundations of the Leadership Formula.

Receiving the right rewards makes followers want to follow. When followers follow with enthusiasm, leaders want to continue to lead. The following syllogism states the concept in a different way:

People who want to lead must have followers.

Followers support people who provide rewards.

Therefore, people who want to become leaders must provide rewards.

Model A shows a typical reward exchange between a manager and a group of employees. It is less than ideal because the employees (at least in their opinion) are providing more rewards than the manager. Under this reward system, employees remain employees.

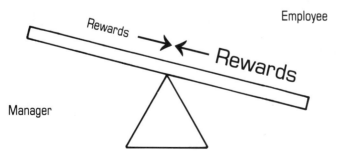

Model B illustrates a better exchange mix. The manager is now a leader and has discovered and is providing more rewards. The balance bar is closer to the middle. Under this reward system, employees often convert themselves from employees into followers.

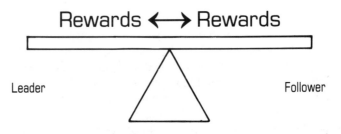

Rewards ⟷ Rewards

Leader   Follower

It must be pointed out that leaders not only provide *more* rewards, they provide more appropriate rewards. And almost all are psychological. Typical rewards are a sense of accomplishment and pride, or a vision that often carries over into the follower's lifestyle, or an *esprit de corps* in the workplace, or hope, self-esteem, and the feeling that comes from being a member of a group that has high standards and status.

GOOD LEADERS PROVIDE PRIMARY REWARDS

Leaders employ their listening skills to search out the "hot buttons," the rewards that followers *really* want (not those that the leaders *think* they want or should have).

A single, highly prized reward is sometimes more valuable than a number of less important rewards. For example, in a city council election, voters might place a much greater value on better police protection than on any other issue. Police protection, therefore, becomes the primary reward; it overshadows less important, possible rewards (better schools, more senior citizen facilities). The candidates who promise better police protection, then, will receive the voters' support.

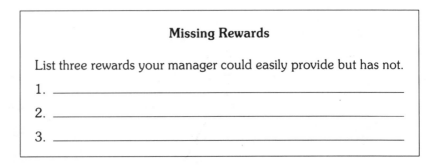

Missing Rewards

List three rewards your manager could easily provide but has not.

1. _____

2. _____

3. _____

Sometimes the primary rewards are the leaders themselves—or the principles or values they represent. Some people will follow leaders because they embody certain ideals or values, not because they offer pragmatic rewards. This is true in all fields, but especially so in politics. Integrity, trust, dependability should be viewed as significant rewards. When people continue to vote for an incumbent because she or he stands for principles those voters admire, then those principles become the reward.

GOOD LEADERSHIP ITSELF IS A VALUED PRIMARY REWARD

Good leadership, then, is the best reward a leader can give to a follower. Nothing can take its place. Good leadership is often perceived by followers as a combination of certain qualities. You will discover many of these by completing the exercise on the following page.

Making MRT work is not easy. It must be accepted as a major challenge. Leaders must provide motivating rewards. They must take into consideration that different followers may want different rewards, and the more followers they have, the more complex the problem becomes.

LEADERS ACCEPT THE CHALLENGE OF CREATING SUPERIOR REWARD SYSTEMS

To discover the right rewards, leaders must be outstanding listeners, sensitive to both the needs of the organization and to the individuals in that organization. They must be able to send rewards to the right target areas at the right time. And then, because they cannot provide all the rewards followers desire, they must decide which rewards make the most sense in view of the situation. It is never a matter of providing all the rewards followers would like, but of providing the best rewards under the circumstances.

Dorothy Dart, the owner of a small electronics firm, called a meeting of her seventeen employees to discuss the rewards she was in a position to provide. She clearly stated that she could provide only one of the two rewards in each of the following categories:

- Higher salaries *or* more fringe benefits.

- She could spend more time with her employees in the plant, *or* she could spend more time developing orders in the field.

- Better working conditions now (costly improvements) *or* a new, far superior shop in the future.

Through open and prolonged discussion, with everyone having a voice, the decision was made to provide more benefits instead of a salary increase, more orders from the field instead of more personal attention, and a new shop in the future instead of improvements now. Once the meeting was over, Ms. Dart knew which rewards to provide. With good follow-through, she can now employ MRT to strengthen her organization and her leadership.

Reward Checklist

Different people look for different rewards from their leaders. Which rewards would you find most satisfying? You can get some indication by completing this exercise. Simply write "1" by your first choice, and so on, until you have written "16" next to the reward that is least important to you. The rewards that please you are probably not very different from those that please your followers.

I would like a leader who

_____   is honest and trustworthy.

_____   is decisive, not wishy-washy.

_____   has the ability to communicate in a clear, forceful manner.

_____   has the strength of character to protect principles important to me.

_____   provides special rewards that are important to me as an individual.

_____   is flexible, who is willing to change when best for followers.

_____   cannot be intimidated by others.

_____   has statesmanlike qualities; that is, someone who thinks of the long-term good and does not get involved in petty issues.

_____   has compassion for others.

_____   is consistent in actions, reliable.

_____   shows interest in my career prospects.

_____   can relax and have fun at the right time.

_____   gives me a compliment when I deserve it.

_____   provides me with learning opportunities.

_____   gives me a sense of pride in what I am doing.

_____   has a personal talk with me now and then.

Add your own:

_____

_____

A leader of a sizable organization who can see that (1) the right personal rewards are provided to his or her immediate staff members, that (2) all other personnel receive adequate personal rewards from their superiors, and that (3) the right general rewards are provided to everyone in the organization is going to have a strong, cohesive, winning organization. The organization will produce more, and everyone will come out ahead. To accomplish this goal, all leaders must develop their own reward matrix according to the goals of the organization and the needs of its members. This, of course, is the crux of the matter. It is one thing to work out an individual mutual reward exchange where both people come out ahead; it is a far greater challenge to work out a group reward exchange where everybody comes out ahead. MRT does, however, offer this opportunity.

The governor of a state might give personal rewards to his (or her) immediate staff and to the members of both houses of the legislature. He must also give general rewards to the voters in the state. The president of a college might concentrate on personal rewards for his (or her) immediate staff, faculty members, and key administrators. General rewards would be provided to students, alumni, and members of the community.

The President of the United States needs to provide his White House staff with the right personal rewards. Such rewards could be anything from the opportunity to be a privileged insider, to personal recognition for a job well done, to backup support when mistakes are made. In return, the President wants complete loyalty, high productivity, and prudent behavior from his staff. The President must also provide general rewards to every citizen (follower) in the country. These, too, must be the right rewards if he wants to be elected again. Primary rewards might be a stronger economy, a more equitable welfare system, or a cleaner environment. *But it must be the right mix of the right rewards at the right time.*

President Eisenhower gave voters some of the key rewards they wanted in the early and mid-fifties. His reputation as a military leader, his Midwestern brand of conservatism, his undeniable patriotism appealed to an electorate worried about the Korean war and the threat of international communism.

Some political observers believe that President Carter, as another example, may have miscalculated the rewards voters wanted when he placed so much emphasis on world peace at the expense of domestic matters. Many people, perhaps more than he and his staff recognized, wanted the reward of a stronger economy and safer cities.

Most followers realize that they are not going to get all the rewards they want, but they want those with high priority to receive first attention. The choice of which rewards to provide (and the relative success at providing them) has a great deal to do with the final ratings Presidents receive in history books.

Followers always determine the destiny of their leaders.

ALL LEADERS MUST DEVELOP THEIR OWN REWARD MATRIX

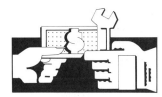

Your Leadership Is Showing

The Presence of Leadership

Rick, the leader of a highly successful rock group for over five years, provided the following rewards to the other four members: good musical arrangements, good bookings, and ample opportunities for individual recognition. In return, his musicians were dependable, made maximum use of their talent, and supported him as their leader in all crucial tests. Rick demonstrated his leadership by insisting that the reward system in operation be discussed openly so that everyone understood the tradeoff involved. When Rick left the group to attend graduate school, the new leader lasted only three months.

Marty discovered quickly that, if her fashion boutique were to survive, she would not be able to pay more than minimum wages to her part-time staff. How could she compensate? She came up with a reward system that doubled her employees' performance. Marty took each employee on a buying trip, took each out for lunch and lots of fashion conversation once a month, and gave each more opportunities to learn about the business. In doing this, she openly discussed how she could provide some rewards and not others. She demonstrated her leadership ability by saying that the best reward she could provide would be to prepare her employees for higher-paying, more demanding fashion jobs elsewhere.

The Absence of Leadership

Joyce was a human resource director for a large branch of a successful retail chain. She reported directly to a corporate vice president. Over a period of three years, Joyce did more than her part in providing all possible rewards to her superior. She researched and introduced some cost-effective procedures; she cut down on personnel turnover; and, most important of all, she solved all these problems without going to the corporate office for help. But Joyce received little recognition from the corporate officer—the one reward she wanted most. As a result, Joyce moved to a competitive company.

Drew was more than upset when he lost his job as restaurant manager. After all, he had majored in restaurant management in college and had devoted seven years of his life to working his way up to manager. Bob Henry, the vice-president, fired Drew because of low morale, low productivity, and excessive customer complaints. Investigation showed that Drew had not provided a good reward system for his employees. His attitude was that if employees did well, he would reward them with a promotion. He demonstrated his lack of leadership by not discovering and providing daily as well as long-term rewards.

PERSONAL VS. GENERAL REWARDS

Personal rewards are rewards a leader gives to either a single follower or a small group of followers. Examples are one-on-one conversations, special attention, and individualized forms of recognition. All leaders can and should provide personal rewards to their immediate staff.

What about leaders who must deal with hundreds, thousands, or millions of followers?

Here the leader must also provide general rewards. A general reward is almost always bestowed impersonally (e.g., in a company memo or an announcement from the dean's office). Needless to say, a general reward must be designed to please the majority of followers. Some obvious examples of general rewards are tax cuts (government), holidays (school administrations), Christmas bonuses (business), and cost-of-living increases (labor).

It is therefore important that top leaders make sure that their subordinates offer personal rewards to those they lead so that everyone in the group receives both personal and general rewards. General rewards, as welcome as they may be, will not replace the need for personal rewards from the immediate leader.

COMMUNICATION AND GENERAL REWARDS

The larger the organization, the more critical is the need for a good delivery network to make certain that rewards reach their destination. In this respect, MRT is dependent upon the quality of the communication systems within the organization. But MRT, if practiced with vigor and sensitivity, can also make a contribution to improving the communication skills of both leaders and followers. Why?

- Making MRT work forces a leader to become a better listener. You simply cannot provide the right rewards until you know what people want. You find these rewards only when you search and listen.

- Setting up a reward system with an individual forces both parties to get together to exchange views, negotiate, and learn more about each other.

- People who must depend upon the media to receive rewards from their leaders listen more and respond better when the leader talks about rewards that are important to them—rewards that are uncovered as a result of research and listening.

The number-one side benefit of MRT is better communication. Leaders should practice it for this alone.

Leaders convert nonfollowers into followers through the way they employ MRT in specific situations. They fail as leaders when they forget to do so. Read the cases on pages 64 and 65. They illustrate what happens when leaders incorporate—or fail to incorporate—MRT into their style.

WHAT REWARDS DO LEADERS RECEIVE?

If MRT is to work, leaders must also receive rewards. In one sense, leaders should not expect as many rewards as followers because certain rewards are automatically built into leadership positions. For example, a psychic payoff takes place the moment one becomes a leader. Some of it comes from follower recognition, but most of it stems from the exercise of power. Most top-level leaders function in an intoxicating environment.

Although highly rewarding, power can be dangerous. Here is a comment from the owner of a manufacturing concern.

> "The heady wine of leadership can send anyone on a disaster trip. The higher the position, the stronger the wine. Beginning leaders must learn to sit on their egos by reminding themselves that leaders are just normal human beings who are supposed to serve their followers and not their own egos. It is not an easy lesson to learn, and as leaders move into more rarified atmospheres, they must learn it over and over again. The problem is one of balance. Leaders must have strong egos to lead; they must also keep thinking well of themselves so they can maintain their personal confidence and continue to lead. But they must eventually learn to live comfortably with the power that is theirs, or their followers will either hope for a fall or actually create it."

Because of the built-in rewards in leadership, leaders should recognize that they will probably give more rewards than they will receive. Leaders should keep in mind that it is sometimes awkward for their subordinates to reward them with more than loyalty and performance. For example, members of the group may want to give their leaders compliments, but because of peer pressure and lack of opportunity, they do not get around to doing so. Leaders who think that their followers are not appreciative should remember two things: If followers had the opportunity, they would probably provide more personal rewards; if they didn't appreciate the leader, they probably would not be following.

None of this is to say that the leader-follower relationship should not be mutually rewarding. It should. It simply states that there is not perfect parity in the mutual reward system.

MRT MOTIVATES BOTH PARTIES

Many definitions of leadership state that a true leader is one who can motivate others. L. L. Bernard gave us this definition in 1926: "Any person who is more than ordinarily efficient in carrying psychological stimuli to others and is thus effective in conditioning collective responses may be called a leader."

Bernard's definition is a simple restatement of what the Mutual Reward Theory is all about. When followers receive the appropriate stimuli (rewards), they in turn reward the leader with a positive response. The process can continue indefinitely. The positive responses of the followers elicit more positive stimuli, which in turn create more positive responses. Everyone comes out ahead.

Followers make leaders when they agree to follow. Followers break leaders when they change their minds. Followers, and followers alone, provide the franchise to lead. Organizations may appoint leaders, but the ultimate source of power comes from followers. Leadership is therefore the ability to attract and keep followers. Unfortunately, all it takes is a few hostile nonfollowers to undermine the power of a leader. That is why leaders must constantly maintain surveillance. When trouble starts, they need to move in quickly and discover the rewards that will get everyone following again.

Ultimately, the Mutual Reward Theory will not work if it is used to strengthen the leader's position at the expense of the followers. Followers soon discover when a leader is self-serving. If rewards, both personal and general, do not have a true ring, they will not be accepted. If MRT is used simply to manipulate followers, it will surely fail.

As one leader commented, "You might be able to manage without a heart, but you cannot lead effectively without one."

THE ULTIMATE FRANCHISE TO LEAD COMES FROM FOLLOWERS

- The Mutual Reward Theory is the human relations foundation for the Leadership Formula.

- MRT will give any leadership style more substance.

- Leaders must constantly monitor, and improve, their reward matrix on behalf of followers.

- It is not only providing the right number of rewards that makes a good leader, it is providing the right rewards.

- Both personal and general rewards must be provided; the further away the leader is from his or her followers, the more important general rewards become.

- The best reward a leader can provide a follower is good leadership; the best reward a follower can provide a leader is productivity.

- The more valuable the rewards, the fewer are required.

- A good way for a leader to restore a relationship with a follower is to discover a better reward system.

- The better the reward system works, the more motivated each party becomes.

- MRT should not be used to manipulate followers in an unfair way.

SUMMARY

Case 9: Compassion

Ralph and Randy are discussing the Mutual Reward Theory on the way home from a religious conference. The theory was introduced by one of the speakers. Ralph is Randy's minister; Randy is an elder.

"Randy," said Ralph, "I'm of the opinion that most good leaders, especially Christians, automatically practice the Mutual Reward Theory."

"I'm not so sure," replied Randy. "In our church, I feel we provide too few rewards to our members and not always the right ones. We lose many members needlessly. For example, the Richardson family left us, and we don't even know why. They were big contributors, too."

"Are you saying that if I and the other leaders of the church would apply the theory that we would serve God better?"

"Yes, I believe that would be true."

"It is too contrived," stated Ralph. "I believe all we need do is demonstrate compassion. When we do this, the rewards are obvious. We don't have to list them."

Randy replied:"I agree that the theory won't work without compassion, but I don't believe compassion will do it alone. We can't build a good reward system without knowing what our congregation wants. We need a more realistic approach if everybody is to come out ahead. For example, I believe it would greatly improve our personal relationship if we could sit down and talk about the rewards we both seek. In a sense, you are the leader and I am the follower. What rewards should I provide? What should I expect from you in return?"

"Perhaps you are right. It might make me a better leader. I'm not so sure, however, that it will be easy for me to do."

Would you recommend that Ralph make a major attempt to weave MRT into his approach as a minister? Because of his compassion for people, would it be easier for him? Would he be more successful? What are the chances, in your opinion, that he will make the behavioral changes necessary? (The author's opinion is in the back of the book.)

Tom Castelletti is the manager of a trucking depot for a large firm. He supervises about sixty truckers and sixteen maintenance people. A high school dropout, he has earned his role as a manager the hard way, starting out as a trucker himself. Bill Nelson, the owner and a strong supporter of Tom, wants him to blend the Mutual Reward Theory into his rough but effective management style. He feels it will improve productivity and create a better relationship with the union. Tom is reluctant to make the move for the following reasons. "The moment I start talking about rewards around here they'll want the sky. The first thing will be more money. Then better hours. It will open up a whole can of worms. The idea may be okay in some places, but not around here. We deal in a more basic way with people. They need more discipline, not less. They would just laugh at this approach."

Case 10: Fear

Bill replies: "Tom, I don't think you get the point. There's nothing to be afraid of. Everyone needs certain rewards from their jobs. Some of these rewards you can provide with little effort if you take the trouble to find out what they are. Others may be beyond your power to provide, and you should just say so. All you are doing now is putting out fires. By working out reward systems with your key people and finding out what the truckers really want, you'll be able to do a much better job with less effort. You'll discover when you open up the subject on a person-to-person basis that the individual will ask for fewer rewards than you suspect. What it boils down to is a kind of relationship contract. If you'll produce for me, I'll do my best to provide the rewards you want. It's a very practical approach."

Bill continues: "I'll tell you what I am willing to do. Let's you and I sit down and work out a better reward system between ourselves. You tell me what rewards you want, and I'll do the same. If it works for us, will you be willing to try it on your truckers?"

Will Bill's approach work? Or are Tom's fears justified? Can MRT work in all environments? (See the back of the book for the author's response.)

Self-Test

Mark each statement True or False.

_____ 1. MRT will add more compassion to any leadership style.

_____ 2. You always know when MRT is working because both parties come out ahead.

_____ 3. A single high-level reward can sometimes equal or replace many smaller rewards.

_____ 4. Generally speaking, leaders provide all the rewards followers need.

_____ 5. Anyone who can make MRT work on a day-to-day basis will substantially improve his or her communication skills.

_____ 6. The ultimate franchise to lead comes from the organization.

_____ 7. MRT is the human relations foundation of the Leadership Formula; if one ignores it, the other foundations are rendered less effective.

_____ 8. Providing the right rewards is often more important than providing a great number of rewards.

_____ 9. MRT is easy to apply.

_____ 10. The best general reward a leader can provide is to be a good leader.

Turn to the back of the book to check your answers.

TOTAL CORRECT _____

Develop Your Power Package

The great principle of all is
that no one of either sex
should be without a
commander.

Plato, Laws XII

**Leaders Know When
and How to Get Tough**

The Mutual Reward Theory is an expression of the human relations side of leadership—the soft side. Structure and discipline are parameters of the other side of leadership—the hard side. The two sides work together. MRT increases the group's tolerance for organizational structure; structure provides the discipline necessary to get the job done. Both are equally important. In fact, one is totally ineffective without the other.

The key to leadership is finding the blend that will work. It is a tightrope every leader and manager must walk daily, as the following example illustrates.

The success of Ruth Reynolds' business college is the talk of the town. Mrs. Reynolds started her school in a dilapidated downtown location seven years ago. Two months ago, the college moved into new, modern facilities to handle a student body which has increased 30 percent a year for three successive years. Why has Mrs. Reynolds been so successful? Perhaps because of her well-balanced blend of personal concern for staff and students and her discipline.

Mrs. Reynolds devotes a great deal of time to MRT counseling—with both staff and students. One of her most common questions is, "What can I do for you that I am not doing already?" But there is never any doubt about who is in charge. She sets a work tempo that others emulate. And if someone does not live up to standards, she intervenes quickly and talks openly about it.

One faculty member made this statement: "She has that rare combination of personal touch and powerful leadership. I never feel neglected or unrewarded, but I also know I must live up to my potential. She can be tough when it's required."

Authority, structure, and discipline are the framework of any successful group or organization. They are the tools of control. They prevent disorganization and chaos.

Without such a framework, there will be squabbles, dissension, and confusion. Any group, no matter what its members might say, needs structure. If provided in the right amount and in the right way, most people welcome and respect it.

Although the words *authority* and *discipline* have a negative connotation for many (because people connect them with a loss of freedom), they should be positive words to would-be leaders. They are the vehicles that will let them express their leadership.

Everyone must, at times, let his or her power show. Authority must be communicated. Structure must be imposed. Timing is important, as the two cases on the next page illustrate.

Everyone was amazed when Jeff received the appointment. He was sensitive to the needs of others and a gifted strategist, but people thought he was too soft to be a head coach. Jeff said little for the first two days, letting people react and adjust. Then he called a meeting of the entire team—players and assistant coaches. He sat on a table and stared at his audience for ten minutes until everyone settled down and decided to listen. Jeff then said: "Everyone in this room has a choice. You must decide whether to accept my authority or drop off the team today. Things will be different around here effective now. We are going to do whatever it takes to put a winning team together. If you are out on the field in ten minutes, I'll know you are with me." He then turned and walked away.

Jeff had, through very few words, expressed his leadership. He drew a line. From that moment on everyone, including the other coaches, would know who was in charge. Jeff was still the nice guy he had always been; but he was now a leader as well.

Lorna Henderson accepted her new position as superintendent of the nursing home knowing that she was walking into a hornet's nest. She spent her first two days being friendly but efficient. On the third day, she scheduled ten-minute private talks with each member of her staff. There was a constant stream of people in and out of her office for six hours. In each interview she made a statement similar to this: "You will find me fair, and I will give you all the rewards and personal time possible. I care about your future, but I have standards that you must live up to. If you do not accept them, I will take corrective action. I intend to turn this nursing home around in sixty days. Once this happens, it will be a much better place for you to work. Are there any questions?"

If leaders do not maintain control, the members of the group begin to go in different directions, and the group becomes fragmented instead of cohesive. If disorder continues, anarchy sets in. The purpose of leadership is to get people to work together toward common goals—to accomplish things that can only be achieved through group effort. The effective leader can make a group achieve more than the sum of its members' individual efforts. None of this can happen, however, without structure. All leaders must at one time or another tighten the reins, stand firm, and take corrective action.

Ralph Stogdill defines leadership as "the initiation and maintenance of structure in expectation and interaction." This definition implies that the leader is responsible for the development of the structure necessary to maximize group performance in the achievement of organizational goals.

MANAGERS AND LEADERS MUST MAINTAIN STRUCTURE

But creating structure and maintaining it does not mean to return to old-fashioned, autocratic forms of leadership. It does not mean harsh, arbitrary rules that subordinates must adhere to or else. It does not mean paternalistic leadership, where all group members are expected to honor their leaders whether they deserve it or not. If a Theory Y leadership style doesn't produce the results a leader anticipated, it does not mean that he or she should embrace Theory X.* MRT and clear, decisive leadership will keep the group headed in the right direction, regardless of leadership style.

There is no escape from the fact that every leader must walk that tight line between freedom and control. The Boy Scout leader must give the members of his troop the freedom to exercise initiative, but exert enough control so that they do not get out of hand. The teacher cannot help students reach learning goals without discipline and respect. The corporate president must run a tight ship in order to reach established productivity and profit goals. Even the President of the United States must occasionally take time to do some corrective counseling with an errant cabinet or staff member. Authority must be expressed. No leader can avoid understanding structure. It goes with the territory.

UNDERSTANDING THE AUTHORITY-LINE CONCEPT

All leaders establish an authority line, an imaginary, psychological demarcation between acceptable and unacceptable behavior. It says to organization members, "I will go along with *this*, but I will draw the line when it comes to *that*." It is a form of communication (perhaps never verbalized) that says, in effect: "You have all the freedom you need to perform effectively and enjoy yourself, but there is a limit. If you go beyond my authority line, you can expect some form of discipline." An authority line can also be interpreted as a stricture that states: "I respect you and your individual rights and will support you enthusiastically, providing you stay within reasonable bounds."

From a group member's point of view, an authority line can be tested: "I will try to get by with as much as possible, even if I step over the line. It won't hurt my progress in the long run." From a leader's point of view, an authority line states: "We have a contract here. I want to provide as much freedom as possible, but I must also maintain control. I am the leader and I must lead. If matters reach a certain point, I will step in. I am willing to

*Theory X, management by control, states that workers must be directed and controlled in order to achieve high productivity. Theory Y, participatory management, states that workers will achieve greater productivity if they can direct their own efforts through involvement with organizational goals.

provide certain rewards, but my return from you is a certain standard of behavior." When a subordinate honors a leader's authority line, the subordinate is giving that leader a reward: accepting his or her leadership.

How and where an authority line is set is a crucial part of anyone's leadership style. It demonstrates how much leadership is present and how sensitive the leader is in employing it.

Is it possible for a leader to draw a line that will be accepted by all group members, provide the structure needed, and help the group reach predetermined goals? If so, must the line be raised or lowered as conditions change?

To answer these questions, let's look at two widely different examples of authority-line violations.

KNOWING WHEN AND WHERE TO DRAW THE LINE

As a manager, for instance, it may not bother you if an employee is occasionally late in returning from lunch—say, fifteen minutes once or twice a week. Your personal tolerance level—related to the authority line you establish—can handle this. But if the same person is twenty minutes late three times a week, you may feel that your tolerance threshold has been crossed, that your authority line has been violated, and some form of discipline is in order. You may say to yourself: "This person does not recognize my leadership role or honor my authority line. My authority is being questioned, and it is time to act. *This person is no longer behaving in a manner I can accept.*"

As a result, you initiate a corrective interview. By taking this action, you have accomplished three things. First, you have used your authority (power) to remind everyone that you have standards. Second, you have adjusted your line as far as recent violations are concerned. Third, and most important, you have clearly expressed your leadership. Although the individual disciplined might react in a negative manner, your other employees might say: "I like the way he leads the department. He doesn't let a few people get away with murder. I just don't like a boss whom people can intimidate." Although readjusting a line may upset violators, it provides necessary group structure. The overall response, at least in the long run, is usually positive.

The President of the United States, in his role as head of the government, establishes a kind of authority line with the Soviet Union. He might state, for example, that if a certain geographical frontier is crossed, a specific action will be taken in response. The United States has a national tolerance level, and once it has been breached (the invasion of an ally), some form of action can be anticipated. The setting and maintenance of authority lines—whether between two leaders or between a leader and a group—is a characteristic of leadership.

If a manager or leader does not take the promised action when his or her authority is violated, the manager or leader loses credibility. A discipline line should not be set in the first place unless it can be upheld. Inactivity or indecision is always interpreted as an absence of leadership.

A common definition of leadership is "the sensitive use of power to achieve group goals." All leaders have power—some more abundantly than others—but it is the way power is exercised that determines whether or not the leader is successful.

Maintaining an Authority Line

There are sensitive and insensitive ways to establish and maintain a clear, firm authority line. A sensitive way protects the self-esteem of the follower so that he or she accepts the message of the leader and *remains a follower.* An insensitive way can turn an enthusiastic follower into a disenchanted employee. Listed below are twelve techniques or approaches frequently used to maintain authority lines. Draw a line through those that you feel will do more harm than good and then match with a classmate or friend.

Ask politely for follower cooperation.

Reprimand violators openly so that everyone gets the message quickly.

Stand tough on previous decisions so everyone knows you mean business.

Communicate strong leadership through image projection; circulate in a friendly manner, but let your bearing indicate that you are in command.

Speak with authority.

Discipline individual violators in private counseling sessions.

Conduct periodic group meetings in which you encourage discussion, but show you are in charge.

Be extra tough on immediate staff, and then delegate maintenance of your authority line to them so that you can appear more benevolent to followers.

Stay with the philosophy that the fewer rules the better, as long as group goals are met. Fewer rules mean less maintenance.

Use the group reprimand approach—if the shoe fits, let the follower wear it.

Take care of violations immediately—before you magnify them out of proportion and before the behavior in question becomes a habit with the violator.

Communicate your displeasure without words—let your negative countenance convey the message.

Power provides the opportunity to be a leader, but it doesn't come with a set of instructions for using it wisely. No warranty is provided. Some leaders fail to use the power they possess; others abuse it; only a few learn to use it skillfully. Establishing an authority line and then protecting it is not the only way a leader expresses power. Power manifests itself in communication, delegation of assignments, and especially in decision making. But nothing impresses subordinates more quickly and clearly than a leader who protects his or her authority line with conviction.

A fundamental difference between managers and leaders is the way they develop and utilize their power. Both may maintain structure and discipline lines, and understand the authority-line concept, but they exercise their power in different ways. To understand how and why this happens, it is necessary to evaluate power sources.

The three basic sources of leadership power are *role power* (the power that goes with the position), *personality power* (power generated by the force of the individual), and *knowledge power* (power that derives from special skills or knowledge).

UNDERSTANDING SOURCES OF POWER

In the exercise of leadership, all sources of power are always present. You cannot rely totally on any single source. But, to gain better follower reaction, it is sometimes best to soft-pedal one source and emphasize another.

A military officer may derive 70 percent of his or her power from the position itself (role power), 20 percent from personality power, 10 percent from expert power. In a combat assignment, the officer's leadership power derives primarily from his rank (role). In a noncombat assignment, his or her expertise or personality might substantially affect, positively or negatively, his or her image as a leader.

In contrast, a minister of a church may derive 50 percent of his or her power from personality, 30 percent from knowledge, and 20 percent from the role itself.

In most cases the power attached to a leadership position is more potent than the person who occupies it realizes. For example, the position of President of the United States has awesome power—no matter who occupies it. To a lesser degree, the same is true of corporate and college presidents, police chiefs, and other government officials. Even the first-line supervisor or volunteer leader has more role power than he or she suspects.

USING ROLE POWER EFFECTIVELY

Power Analysis

Although all leaders make use of all three power sources, some positions call for more emphasis on one source than another. (Also, there is the shifting of power sources according to the situation.) What, in your opinion, would be a reasonable percentage breakdown of the power sources in these leadership roles?

	Lab Manager	Movie Director	Girl Scout Leader
Role Power	_____%	_____%	_____%
Personality Power	_____%	_____%	_____%
Knowledge Power	_____%	_____%	_____%
	100%	100%	100%

If you rated knowledge power high (perhaps 60 percent) for the lab manager, role power high for the movie director, and personality power high for the Girl Scout leader, you would be on the right track.

Role power is generally accepted without question. People know it is not easy to be in a position of authority; in fact, they are often sympathetic to those who are. (How often have you heard someone say about the President, "I wouldn't have his job if they paid me a million dollars a year!") People, however, do not react well to leaders who abuse power. They resent the coach, the senator, the boss who takes advantage of the power engendered by his or her position. The coach who bullies his players, the senator who doesn't vote on key issues, the boss who betrays his employees' trust will soon find themselves without followers.

Generally speaking, the best way to use role power is to let it work silently. Live with that power comfortably and use it gracefully. Recognize it, but don't let it go to your head.

Role power, however, is there to be used and should be communicated without hesitation under certain circumstances—for example, when an authority line needs to be lowered. No other source of power will reestablish the leader's authority more quickly, as the following examples illustrate.

"Frank, the difference between you and me is that I am sitting in the chair of the president. You don't have to like me as a person, but you must respect my position. From now on I expect you to conform to policy like everyone else."

"Okay, everybody. We made excellent progress last month, but we still need to eliminate some safety violations. Keep in mind that my position forces me to take disciplinary action if necessary. The same would be true if you had my job."

"There is nothing personal about it, but as long as I occupy this position, that's the way it will be. No exceptions."

> **GENERALLY SPEAKING, LEADERS ARE GENTLE IN THE USE OF ROLE POWER. THEY DOWNPLAY THE SOURCE. WHEN THEY DO USE IT, THEY DRAW A FIRM LINE AND QUICKLY MOVE ON TO THE UTILIZATION OF OTHER SOURCES.**

USING PERSONALITY POWER

Every individual—whether in a leadership role or not—has personality power. We can all use our personalities to influence others. Those who have a positive attitude, a pleasant voice, a decisive manner, and a strong sex identity frequently have the most impact.

Charisma is a word that we hear frequently today. Some leaders have it in abundance; others have none. Movie stars who have it are winners at the box office; politicians who do not have it may find it difficult to get elected. But what is it?

Webster's *New World Dictionary* defines *charisma* as "a special quality of leadership that captures the popular imagination and inspires unswerving allegiance and devotion." Charismatic people apparently have a star quality that makes people want to follow them. Charisma is great for those who possess it. If you do not have it, however, it does not mean that you have no personality power.

You do.

Personality power becomes important in positions of leadership that are inherently weak in role power. For example, many teachers recognize that their role as classroom leader does not have high power content, so they tap their personality power more heavily. They do not say, "Look, I'm the teacher so what I say goes." Rather, they skillfully employ their personality power to achieve higher learning levels. This is true of many leadership roles—volunteer leaders, ministers, elected leaders in trade, fraternal, and social organizations. They get more voltage from the power of their personalities than from the roles they occupy.

Leadership and Charisma

Rate the following Presidents (on a scale of one through ten) on their leadership ability and charisma.

Leadership		Charisma
_____	Harry Truman	_____
_____	Dwight Eisenhower	_____
_____	John Kennedy	_____
_____	Lyndon Johnson	_____
_____	Richard Nixon	_____
_____	Gerald Ford	_____
_____	Jimmy Carter	_____
_____	Ronald Reagan	_____

Study your ratings. Is there any correlation—either positive or negative—between leadership and charisma? What conclusions can you draw about the role charisma plays in the development of leadership qualities?

The 1980 National Democratic Convention provided an excellent contrast in the use of role versus personality power. President Carter leaned heavily on his role as President and head of the Democratic Party, whereas Senator Kennedy leaned heavily on his personality power. The leadership profiles communicated were different because the power sources were different.

When a "power personality" occupies a "power role," you always have the possibility of outstanding leadership, provided that both power sources are used effectively.

IN MOST CASES, LEADERS USE THEIR PERSONALITY POWER TO INSPIRE AND PERSUADE FOLLOWERS. MANAGERS, ON THE OTHER HAND, FALL BACK ON THEIR ROLE POWER TO ACHIEVE PRODUCTIVITY.

When a leader has special skills and knowledge to back up the leadership role he or she occupies, an additional source of power is generated. This is *knowledge power*. People like to be led by those who know the answers. They look up to those with expertise, giving them more authority than they would otherwise possess. Knowledge—real or imagined—is power.

MAKING THE MOST OF KNOWLEDGE POWER

Being recognized as an expert gives you additional clout. For example, a major who went to West Point is generally more respected than one who graduated from Officers Candidate School. A president of a genetic engineering company who has a Ph.D. in biochemistry is listened to more closely than one who studied business. True expertise, then, generates power automatically.

Sometimes, knowledge power can be more important than any other kind. For example, the pilot of an airliner is the captain (role power); he or she may have a strong personal presence (personality power); but it is the ability to fly the plane safely that is the source of the pilot's primary power. In a rough sky, skill is what counts—not the title or charm the pilot may possess.

Leadership itself is expertise.

Many times leadership skills are valued more highly than technical competence. In fact, in most high-level leadership roles one is more likely to find people with leadership skills than technical competence. The best engineer in the world cannot run an engineering firm without leadership ability. The winning combination, of course, is leadership capabilities and technical knowledge.

The primary danger for those who possess expertise is relying on it too heavily. The know-it-all leader soon loses both friends and followers. The leader who refuses to listen is quickly in trouble. But the leader who has both technical expertise and leadership ability has a definite edge. Sometimes knowledge can be the primary source of power, as this case illustrates:

> Brenda majored in mathematics and minored in computer science in college. It turned out to be a perfect combination because she was hired by a computer manufacturer the day after graduation. In less than two years, Brenda was offered a job with a client organization. The board of the client company wanted someone to manage those who were going to operate the computer equipment they had bought from Brenda's firm. She took the job, at a big jump in pay and a drop in status. She was given the title of acting manager, which diminished her role power. On top of this, Brenda was a rather quiet, unassuming, work-oriented person. She would be the first to admit that she had little personality power. So Brenda relied heavily—almost 90 percent—on her knowledge of what she was doing.

It didn't take long for those in her department to sense how lucky they were to have her as an acting manager. She seemed to be able to come up with the solution to any computer or programming problem. In addition, she was a great teacher. She always took time to explain how things operate and why it was wiser to do something one way than another. Because of her knowledge (and her ability to communicate it), Brenda earned the respect of her subordinates without having a great deal of role or personality power.

It wasn't long before Brenda was appointed manager of the computer center (no longer acting), and after a while she became more confident because of the positive feedback she received from the people in her department. But even after she gained more role and personality power, she was respected (and followed) primarily because of her knowledge. She had, for that department at least, the right blend of power for a leadership style.

Technical and scientific experts, as well as other specialists, are often short on personality power. Many a research and development person has been promoted into a leadership role, only to request a transfer back to the laboratory or design bench. Many an outstanding salesperson has tried the role of sales manager, only to return to the field. In such cases, it is usually a failure to understand or use the elements that make a power base.

> ALTHOUGH LEADERS AND MANAGERS MAY HAVE
> THE SAME LEVEL OF KNOWLEDGE POWER,
> LEADERS OFTEN SPEND MORE TIME
> TEACHING FOLLOWERS WHAT THEY KNOW.
> IN DOING THIS, THEY GAIN GREATER RESPECT,
> LOYALTY, AND PRODUCTIVITY.
> MANAGERS SEEM TO TAKE THEIR KNOWLEDGE
> FOR GRANTED; THUS, THEY SHARE IT LESS.

POWER PACKAGE UTILIZATION PROFILES

A typical power package utilization profile for managers might approximate the one illustrated below. You will observe that many managers, perhaps most, rely heavily on their role power. A few consider it their only power source. In contrast, many apparently fail to develop their personality power. Some, perhaps because they lack self-confidence, permit their personality power to dry up under the details, procedures, and red tape associated with the management marshmallow. Even knowledge power is ignored by some managers, when, in fact, they have more power than leaders in comparable roles. A few managers render themselves less effective because they do not "keep up" with developments. When this happens, respect often disintegrates.

Manager

A typical power package utilization profile for a successful leader is more apt to approximate the following. Many leaders try not to use their role power, believing it may have a more negative impact on followers than personality power. These leaders claim that people are more willing to accept personality power than the raw power that comes from occupying a position. Leaders with charisma obviously make the most of their

Leader

personalities. Some leaders, but not all, make better use of knowledge power than do managers. Not only do they try to keep ahead of followers in technical data, but they do a superior job of teaching what they know and communicating in general.

Although managers and leaders alike can benefit from a periodic review of how they are utilizing their power package, those who feel boxed in as managers might free themselves by revamping their profiles along the lines of the typical leader. In doing this, however, they should be careful to strike a "balance" within their comfort zone.

The best way to use the power inherent in your role is to occupy your position with ease, grace, and confidence. Power goes with the role, but your projection of "presence" either increases or decreases your authority.

You increase your personality power by learning how to capitalize on your strong traits and strengthening your weak ones.

You increase your knowledge power by learning more about the technology and skills in your special area. The more you know, the more you will be able to communicate to subordinates. The more knowledge you communicate, the more respect (and power) they will give you.

In any situation, all power sources available to the leader are drawn upon. They cannot be clearly separated. The leader, however, can often be more effective if he or she uses one source of power rather than another. To provide practice in how different power sources might be emphasized in different situations, the following exercise has been developed. Please read the situation first, then select the one or two sources of power you feel would best accomplish the task at hand with as little negative reaction as possible.

Power Source Exercise

Listed below are twelve situations in which one power source (or perhaps two equal power sources) might be most effective. The author has checked his preferences. If you agree, place a check in the appropriate square. If possible, have a friend make his or her selections so that a discussion can take place.

Situation	Role Power	Personality Power	Knowledge Power	Agree
1. Insubordination by an employee in a nuclear power plant	☑	☐	☐	☐
2. Retraining an older employee to operate a new-generation computer	☐	☑	☑	☐
3. Motivating a staff employee whose productivity has dropped dramatically	☐	☑	☐	☐
4. Lowering the authority line on all subordinates because of infractions by a few	☑	☐	☐	☐
5. President of United States giving a State of the Union address to Congress (and the country via television)	☐	☑	☑	☐
6. Minister appearing before congregation to ask for financial pledges	☐	☑	☐	☐
7. Manager using MRT to counsel a valued employee who has been acting hostile recently	☐	☑	☐	☐
8. Announcing discovery of a theft ring and a plan to combat recurrence	☑	☐	☐	☐
9. Selling the need for a new piece of technical equipment to your superiors	☐	☑	☑	☐
10. Announcing a layoff in your organization	☑	☑	☐	☐
11. College president appearing before faculty for the first time	☐	☑	☑	☐
12. Police chief speaking before graduating class of police academy	☑	☑	☐	☐

INCREASING YOUR POWER BASE

Managers and leaders can increase their power base regardless of their situation. The first possibility, of course, is promotion into a more powerful role. Increasing one's personality power is a more personal matter. Although courses in communication, public speaking, and self-analysis are helpful, personality enhancement can be a do-it-yourself project. And increasing one's knowledge power can be accomplished on campus, as one earns a higher degree; on the job, through seminars and work projects; and individually, through self-study. Although successful managers strive to increase their power base, leaders often make a greater effort in this direction. They know that the stronger their power base, the more leadership they can put into their style.

Followers study their leaders carefully and are more sensitive to how leaders use power than the leaders realize. Although group members may not respond immediately to their leader's use, or abuse, of power (they may be busy adjusting to a new authority line or working harder to reach a group goal), the image they form of the leader is, in large part, determined by the way he or she handles power.

This is an important factor when you consider that the ultimate source of a leader's power is the people he or she leads.

SUMMARY

- The sensitive application of MRT makes the addition of structure more acceptable to employees and followers.

- Without structure, organizations start to fall apart and productivity drops.

- Whether a manager or leader, where you set your authority line is important; the way you maintain it is critical.

- A typical manager's power package utilization profile is often different from that of a leader.

- Some managers don't develop their personality power.

- Some managers and leaders do not fully utilize their knowledge power.

- Leaders and managers can improve their power base.

Jane and Gloria are unlikely friends. Jane is a small, quiet, timid woman of thirty-six whose marriage has recently fallen apart. She has returned to college in an effort to find a career that will help her put her life back together. Gloria is a powerful personality who operates a successful health spa. They met when Jane joined Gloria's spa.

One evening, after closing the club, Jane and Gloria stopped in a nearby coffee shop. Jane began to talk about Gloria's behavior that night.

"Gloria, I'm amazed at how you can stand up for yourself when somebody starts to get out of line. Like tonight, you really put that John Spencer in his place. How can you do this?"

"In my opinion, leadership is 90 percent guts. Every once in a while, I actually look for an opportunity to get tough. Afterward, things go better."

"I wish I were more like you. Frankly, I'll never be a leader—I just don't have the courage. I've been a follower all my life, so I guess I'll stay one."

"Anybody can be a leader if they really want to. I'm looking for an assistant right now. If you let me train you, you can have the job. I can give you the confidence you need to step out and run things when I'm gone."

Do you believe Gloria can convert Jane into a leader? Or are some people born to be followers? Defend your position. (And then turn to the back of the book to discover the author's position.)

Case 11: Courage

Case 12: Compatibility

Major Brokaw and Captain Small are attending the same military leadership seminar. Major Brokaw has almost thirty years of service. Captain Small has less than ten. They are discussing the problem of blending the Mutual Reward Theory and additional structure together.

"So far I'm not impressed with the formula proposed by our instructor. I understand MRT, but I think it is a weak approach. If I start out with such a soft human relations approach and then suddenly add more discipline, I'll be in trouble. It's like trying to mix oil and water. I believe the rewards one can get in the military are self-evident. Can you imagine me sitting down with a corporal and asking what rewards he expects from me?"

"Yes, I can," replied Captain Small. "I think it would be a good investment of your time. You'd discover what rewards are required these days to build motivation. And I think you would learn a great deal about yourself."

"Okay. I might give it a try. But I still can't see how MRT and more structure go together. To me, they are just not compatible."

"On the contrary. In my opinion, the more you use MRT, the more structure your men will accept. You see, you start out on a human basis, and once your men know that you will give them certain rewards, then they will accept discipline more readily. It's the combination that works. When you use MRT first, you set the stage for more structure, not the other way around."

Captain Small continues. "We sure see things differently. I don't think of MRT as a weak approach. Just good sense. As a leader, I have a contract with the men under my command. The better the contract, the better the relationship, and the better the relationship, the more I can expect from them under stress. I want them to accept my orders when they are necessary. That's why I use MRT."

Do you agree or disagree with Captain Small? Are MRT and structure more compatible in some environments than others? Do you agree that those leaders who do a good job with MRT will be able to apply more structure without getting resistance? Is it possible to be a compassionate leader in the modern military establishment? (Read the author's reaction in the back of the book.)

Mark each statement True or False.   # Self-Test

_____ 1. The more MRT is used, the more structure subordinates will accept.

_____ 2. Structure without MRT can be counterproductive.

_____ 3. Role power is personality based.

_____ 4. Leaders expand utilization of role power and diminish use of knowledge power.

_____ 5. Scientists make excellent leaders because they have more knowledge power.

_____ 6. Overemphasis of one source of power and neglect of others can injure the leader's image.

_____ 7. Charisma is part of personality power.

_____ 8. All successful leaders have charisma.

_____ 9. Managers and leaders utilize personality power at the same level.

_____ 10. One of the best ways to demonstrate more leadership is to provide more structure.

Turn to the back of the book to check your answers.

TOTAL CORRECT _____

Make Better Decisions More Decisively

Not to decide is to decide.

Harvey Cox

**Leaders Welcome
Decision Making as an
Opportunity to Express
Their Leadership**

A chartered plane, flying over dense jungle, crashes. Both pilots are killed. The forty passengers, unharmed but in shock, wonder how to get back to civilization. None of the passengers has had jungle survival training. Through the group process, they decide that their chances of survival will be greater if they stick together and choose a single, strong leader.

What kind of a person should they choose?

Many factors come to mind, but far above the most important personal quality is the ability to make good decisions. Which direction should the party take? What about food and water? Shelter from the elements? Protection from jungle insects? The moment a leader is chosen, he or she must make decisions quickly and with authority.

In any and all leader-follower situations good decision making eventually surfaces as a characteristic followers value highly. Leaders say the same thing in many ways.

"Poor decision making is the downfall of most leaders."

"Decision making is a symbol of leadership."

"It's not just making good decisions, it's making them with authority and decisiveness."

"Every decision I make has something to do with the health of my corporation. It's when I make these decisions that I know I'm the leader."

"Making decisions is the most demanding thing I do."

"I get paid plenty for being a leader, but it's only when I make a hard decision that I know I have earned it."

"I'm accepted as the leader of this organization because I have been able to take it in the right direction. They may not vote for me on a popularity basis, but they respect me as a decision maker. That is why I remain their leader."

The rank and file also agree that decision making should be an integral part of the Leadership Formula.

"We are totally dependent on the quality of decisions made at the top. If they are bad, we all get hurt."

"It is certainly easy to follow a leader with charisma, but if the leader doesn't make the right decisions, my job is on the line."

"You quickly lose respect for a leader who can't make good decisions."

"There is nothing more frustrating than having to work for someone who can't make up their mind."

When a coach makes superior decisions, players win games and feel good about their leadership. When a mayor makes good decisions, the quality of life in the city improves. When a corporate president makes the right decisions, everyone who works for the company benefits.

MAKING GOOD DECISIONS INCREASES YOUR FOLLOWERSHIP

There is a classic example of the importance of good decision making from the world of business. After World War II, Montgomery Ward, under the leadership of Sewell Avery, decided to retrench and conserve capital until after a predicted recession had passed. Sears Roebuck, on the other hand, decided to expand, sensing that a boom period was around the corner. As a result, Sears became the number-one retailer in the world while Ward lost ground. Everyone connected with Sears developed the feeling of pride that comes from playing on a winning team. Good decisions had earned their support.

Everyone can and should contribute, where possible, to the decision-making process. In the final analysis, however, leaders make the critical decisions. The burden is theirs.

Our dependence on the decision-making ability of our leaders cannot be overestimated. For example, President Harry Truman was forced into making some tough decisions while in office. We are still living with the atomic bomb decision. The destiny of any group, organization, or country lies with the decisions made by its leader. There is no escape.

If you improve your decision making, you will increase your power and add more leadership to your management style.

IMPROVING YOUR DECISION MAKING PROCESS

Decision making has never been easy. It never will be. Leaders who can communicate well, use MRT sensitively, and exercise power wisely may ultimately fail because of poor decision making. Even those who are good at it make a few bad decisions that come back to haunt them. No one bats 1000.

How can you improve your average? First, follow these three steps and then develop a process that fits your style and comfort zone.

1. Sit down in a quiet place alone. Do not make major decisions on the run or under pressure.

2. Clear all distracting elements from your mind. Good decisions require concentration.

3. Using a pencil, devise a process similar to the one in "A Decision-Making Formula."

A Decision-Making Formula

The purpose of this model is to show how the decision-making process works. First, read the entries under the column titled "Process." Note that there is one step for each letter in the word *decisions*. Next, read the entries under "Instructions" so that you will be able to apply the process to any decision you make in the future.

Process	*Instructions*
Define desired outcome.	You need to know exactly what you want to accomplish before you can decide the best way to do it.
Establish decision criteria.	What are the guideposts? For example, if you were deciding whether to drive or take the bus to work, you would consider factors like wear and tear on your car, safety, cost, and time saved.
Come up with alternative solutions.	Write out all possible courses of action that will lead to the desired outcome.
Investigate—get all possible facts.	Accumulate as many facts as time permits. List them on a separate sheet of paper.
Settle on top three choices.	List them.
Instigate a comparison.	Weigh the three choices and decide among them. Consult with others if necessary.
Opt for the best choice.	List your final decision.
Notify those involved with decisiveness.	The way you articulate your decision can be as important as the quality of the decision itself. Write how you intend to announce it.
See that decision is fully implemented.	A good decision must be made to work. Write out how you intend to do this.

THE MORE LOGIC THE BETTER

Do leaders actually follow models like the one illustrated each time they make a decision? Do they always stop, clear their minds, and then proceed, step by step, through a structured procedure? Most do not, but those who rely heavily on some form of logical process make better decisions.

In the first place, few leaders ever find a single procedure that is always reliable. Most experiment with a number of approaches, constantly attempting to improve their skills. Second, decision makers seem to select different procedures (if they use any at all) for different kinds of problems. For example, they might follow a structured pattern for a major problem, a more intuitive pattern for a minor one.

Finally, and perhaps most important, there is not always time for a formal step-by-step analysis of problem situations. As one leader stated,

> "Despite all the computer data available to me, I must still make most decisions in my guts. I just don't have time to gather and fully analyze all the facts. Things are moving too fast. There are too many emergencies."

But every leader should, when possible, follow a logical pattern to improve the quality of decisions. Leaders who do reduce the risk of making bad decisions. Our model shows what some experts might consider an ideal process under ideal conditions. You may never find an "ideal condition," but eventually you need to develop a process that works for you. This may be, as most leaders claim, a never-ending search that will always require adjustments and improvements to fit the situation. But the effort must be made.

CLARITY OF THINKING

It stands to reason that clear thinking is required for good decision making. A muddled mind will not make a clear decision. No argument here. For many decision makers, time and place have a great deal to do with clear thinking. Some people claim they think more clearly early in the morning, after a good night's sleep and before the daily pressures pile up. Others say that they must get away to another environment to sort things out more clearly. A growing number of executives claim that running produces a "clarity of thinking" that can produce better decisions. Each individual needs to experience many decision-making climates to discover the one that works best.

Obviously, anything a decision maker can do to clear his or her head for thinking is worth doing.

INDECISION IS A BAD DECISION

Leaders must be careful not to spend so much of their time perfecting their decision-making systems that they cannot provide direction when it is needed. When there is indecision, organizations become fragmented and employees scramble in different directions.

> Everyone had high hopes for the new university president. He was a disciplined academician, an accomplished writer, a good communicator, and an outstanding manager. But it soon became apparent that he could not make hard decisions quickly. In fact, the backlog of problems requiring major decisions nearly brought the university to a standstill. For example, in a time of increasing enrollments he

refused to trim the fat from his administrative staff and hire more teachers, which resulted in heavier classroom loads for his already overburdened teaching staff. This eventually caused a faculty rebellion. When his four-year contract was up, the university was in a shambles.

Hudson T. Armerding, president of Wheaton College, made the following statement in his book *Leadership**: "I prefer someone who acts—even if he makes mistakes on occasion. I believe that if he is 51 percent right in his actions, he is performing more satisfactorily than if he does nothing."

Sweeping problems under the rug is abdicating the leadership role. Good or bad, decisions must be made.

Not only should decisions be made within a reasonable length of time, they should be made with decisiveness. A decision, no matter how small it may be, should show the presence of leadership.

Smart leaders capitalize on opportunities to announce decisions they feel good about. You hear them saying something to this effect: "I am proud to make this announcement. This decision takes our organization in the right direction. All of us will come out ahead."

In announcing a decision, leaders should use their role power to set the stage and gain the attention of followers, their personality power to present the decision in the best light, and their knowledge power to communicate why the decision is a good one, based upon the facts.

DECISION MAKING AND IMAGE

Despite the fact that the rank and file may not always appear interested in the decisions their leaders make, there is a high correlation between the ability to make decisions and the image a leader projects.

Greg made a hard decision when three of his key players were caught using drugs. They were suspended from the team for the season. A tough decision, but the rest of the players, as well as school officials, recognized it as the right one. Although they lost the next few games, the team got into the playoffs. The following year Greg discovered he had more support from players, administrators, and parents than ever before. His image had been enhanced.

Victoria, who was the city's recreation director, recommended closing the downtown swimming pool when it became obvious that there was not enough money to keep all three city pools open. Besides, she argued, the downtown pool, which was used primarily by poor minorities, was a big source of trouble. Victoria underestimated the reaction from the community, and within ten days she

---

*Published by Tyndale House, Wheaton, Ill., 1978.

had to withdraw her recommendation. As a result of her ill-advised decision, her image was damaged, and she knew it.

When a leader makes a decision that most people will react positively to, he or she should see that the message is widely broadcast. It can only enhance the leader's image. On the other hand, if an unpopular decision must be made, it should be soft-pedaled. When a leader makes a bad decision (and discovers it in time), he or she can only hope that it will not receive too much publicity—assuming, of course, that this leader has some control over the media. This is not always the case. When leaders in the public sector make serious mistakes, the prying eye of the media will generally uncover them. Sometimes public reaction can destroy a leader.

All leaders wind up making a bad decision now and then, and generally everybody finds out about it. When this happens, it is the way in which leaders live with that decision that determines their real leadership capabilities. Those who quickly admit they made a mistake and openly attempt to repair the damage usually come out ahead.

LIVING WITH A BAD DECISION

> Raymond was dean of student activities for a large university. When he discovered that a few football players had been given credit for courses they did not attend, he made the decision to keep the discovery to himself, but to make sure the practice was stopped immediately. Later, because of an NCAA investigation, it all came out. Raymond quickly admitted he had made the wrong decision and apologized to the administration and to the student body. He made no further attempts to cover up. Although some damage was done to his image, he survived the investigation and, at least in the eyes of a few people, wound up with more stature than he had before.

It is not easy to live with a bad decision. It can destroy confidence and cause the decision maker to be indecisive in the future. Additionally, it can undermine anyone's faith in his or her ability to make good decisions.

> Helen knew she had made a mistake the second day after she had appointed Rick her assistant. He did nothing but rub everyone the wrong way. Productivity slumped. As a result, she lost confidence in her ability to make good decisions, and things went from bad to worse. When it was all over—and she had resigned—Helen decided she did not want any kind of leadership role in the future. Decision making was not her cup of tea.

A few bad decisions do not a poor leader make. A leader's overall image counts more than his or her won/loss record. Nobody keeps records anyway. One way to compensate for a bad decision is to quickly make good decisions that neutralize or offset the bad one.

> When Sam discovered that he had made a serious mistake by recommending that his firm establish a legal clinic in the city of Cypress, he made a series of other decisions to offset his mistake. First, he admitted that his site research had been faulty. Second, he quickly closed the clinic and announced that he had been able to sublet the building to the advantage of the firm. Third, he worked up new procedures for making better site selections in the future. These new decisions helped to compensate for the damage the first decision did to his image. He also showed strong leadership by demonstrating that he could handle mistakes without losing confidence in himself.

DECISION REVERSALS

Decision reversals are common, and they have less impact upon the leader's image than one might expect. Many leaders told me that, in their opinion, they lose far less respect when they openly reverse a bad decision than when they let it simmer. Apparently the rank and file have a higher tolerance for bad decisions than most people suspect, as this quotation implies:

> "I believe most followers view their leaders as they do their favorite baseball players. They do not expect their leaders to bat 1000 on decision making. Not that they don't hold their leaders accountable, they do; but they don't expect the impossible."

Decision making may be a primary criterion for superior leadership, but no one expects miracles. People want clear decisions; they want quick decisions; and they want decisions that are good for the organization and themselves. And if a bad decision is made, they want their leaders to acknowledge their part in it, and then do something about it before everyone is hurt even more. *A reversal is far more acceptable than a bad decision that is allowed to remain in force.*

DECISION FLIP-FLOPS DESTROY LEADERSHIP IMAGE

A leader who makes a serious mistake and then corrects it is forgiven. But the leader who reverses a decision because of pressure from special-interest groups is respected by no one. It is true that the best decision is the one that benefits everyone, but even when it is impossible to please all subgroups, a decision must be made. Once the best decision has been made, it is wise to stick with it even though not everyone is happy. Leaders who permit pressure from one group to cause them to flip-flop on a decision usually wind up making everyone unhappy.

Progressive organizations have strengthened themselves by taking the time to involve employees in those decisions that affect them the most. Employees gain ego satisfaction from being involved and are more apt to be enthusiastic about decisions they have participated in. Morale improves. There are two situations in which involving subordinates is especially wise. One, when you as a leader need more information. Two, when it is necessary to eliminate resistance to whatever the ultimate decision will be.

But the dangers of rank-and-file involvement sometimes outweigh the advantages. If the process takes too long, the decision may be delayed (and the leader accused of indecisiveness). Another danger is involving some subordinates and not others, creating dissension and divisiveness in the ranks. The biggest danger of all is that the group will come up with a "committee" decision, one so full of compromises that it is less effective than the one the leader could have made alone. Then the leader is involved in a no-win situation. He or she must either go along with the decision or override it. If the leader overrides it, the problems that result will probably be much greater than those created by living with it.

Time permitting, democratic decision making can produce outstanding results. In many situations it is the best approach to take. On the other hand, too much consultation communicates leadership weakness. The right balance is hard to achieve.

DECISION MAKING AND THE GROUP PROCESS

Choosing the wrong staff member has caused the downfall of more leaders than any other factor. It is, beyond question, the most important area of decision making. And the more often a leader needs to add a new staff member or replace an old one, the more chance there is to make a mistake.

Why is it so difficult to select enthusiastic, capable, loyal staff members? The primary reason appears to lie in the premise that a leader needs staff members who are a reflection of his or her leadership style. In other words, when you ask someone to be a member of your inner circle, you are, in effect, saying: "I am asking you, as a staff member and follower, to support my policies and leadership style so that we can present a united front and image to outside followers. Within our circle, we can express our differences openly. In return, I will do my best to provide you with all rewards, both personal and professional."

Trouble often seems to start with a difference in opinion, based upon a conflicting set of values. But the root of the problem is apt to be a difference in style. When one can no longer feel comfortable in a staff role for a leader, time seldom produces a solution. The best thing for both parties is for the staff member to resign; the worst thing is for the staff member to initiate critical infighting and, eventually, become disloyal.

SELECTION OF STAFF: THE MOST CRITICAL DECISION

Why do leaders often seem to have blind spots in selecting their staff? Perhaps they project their own image into the behavior of another; perhaps they see only what they want to see; perhaps they fail to employ the process and skills they would normally use in other types of decisions. Although no leader can be expected to bat even close to 1000, three suggestions could improve the staff-selection batting average of some leaders.

1. *Ask for a second opinion.*   Few leaders have had extensive personnel and interviewing experience; so they, more than others, need professional advice in this area. Leaders should seek honest opinions from objective people (already onboard), listen carefully, and then make a decision. Slowing down the selection process is a good idea.

2. *Discuss your leadership style with candidates.*   Explain why you need staff members who will be an extension of your style and not their own. Admit that there is a "conformity price" to be paid as far as projecting an external image is concerned. Then discuss the advantages and how MRT can apply. Give an applicant time to assess the invitation.

3. *Interview at least three applicants (in depth) for each replacement.*   Complete the research on each person before you extend an invitation. Satisfy yourself that the selected individual will become a team member and contribute to the productivity, enthusiasm, and enjoyment of other staff members.

Even after you've taken all precautions, a mistake can be made. When this happens, take immediate action to remedy the situation. Follow all the principles of MRT, the law, and recognized procedures—but *act.* Your future role as a leader will depend upon it!

COURAGE AND DECISION MAKING

Courage and leadership are first cousins. Insecure people who are always looking for ways to protect themselves, or who prefer to stay out of the limelight, do not become good leaders. People who will do anything to keep people liking them do not become effective leaders. People who avoid controversy at all costs do not become long-term leaders.

Courage means taking a stand that is not popular but is best for the group. It means making a tough decision, knowing you might be proved wrong at a later date. It means saying no to someone you like, knowing that he or she may turn against you in the future. It means risking rejection by people you care about, because you must make an unpopular decision.

Generally speaking, people who postpone making a difficult decision do so because they lack the courage to make it. Those who form committees and ask for recommendations (when they already have the facts) are often delaying decisions to get themselves off the hook. All leaders must make some hard decisions, and making them usually takes guts. There is no escape.

EMOTIONAL STRENGTH— A NECESSITY

Leaders recognize that some isolation from their subordinates, even members of their staff, is part of the role they play. (It is indeed often lonely at the top.) This means that leaders must rely heavily on their own strengths and resources.

Leaders who have emotional strength stay calm in turmoil. They handle stress without becoming too discouraged. They handle outside criticism without taking it too personally. Only subordinates enjoy the luxury of relaxing under the protective umbrella of the organization; they can, for the most part, exempt themselves from stress.

Leaders cannot become part of the crowd. They must take defeat and bounce back. They must live through traumatic reversals. They must accept the fact that leaders are not always popular. They must learn to live with the fact that both their actions and their words will be misinterpreted.

STAGING DECISION ANNOUNCEMENTS

Have you noticed how political and corporate leaders use the media to stage announcements of major decisions? Even in much smaller ways (and probably without media help), staging major announcements is a good idea for all leaders. Here's why.

1. Followers who hear about a decision affecting them directly from the leader are apt to support it. Especially is this true if the announcement is made with fanfare and decisiveness.

2. The sooner followers know about a decision that impacts upon them, the better. Delays can cause ugly rumors.

3. A well-staged announcement becomes a positive force and can enhance one's leadership image. Followers need to see, hear, and react in a positive way to "leaders of the pack."

Whatever your position (only a few leaders have media access), do everything you can to stage the announcement of a major decision. Have your staff set the stage, try for the largest audience, and use your best platform manner to deliver a positive announcement. Use all the showmanship possible, as long as it falls within your comfort zone.

A FINAL WORD

Putting more leadership into your style through better, sharper decision making is a do-it-yourself project. The effort, however, is worth it. Success will earn you greater respect from those who are dependent on your leadership, because good decision making is tantamount to a reward they will appreciate. Good decisions will either keep you in your leadership role or open the door to a better one!

SUMMARY

- Leaders and followers agree that good decision making is a primary criterion for successful leadership.

- Most people can improve their decision-making skills by a system or procedure that employs logic. However, a procedure can only *lead* to a better decision; it cannot make it.

- Leaders are respected when they make the best decision in a quick, decisive manner.

- Staff personnel decisions are the most critical of all.

- Leadership is often signaled as much by the way a decision is announced as by the decision itself.

- There is a high correlation between good decision making and the kind of leadership image that is signaled.

- The group decision-making process should be followed as long as it leads to good decisions.

- It is better to correct a bad decision than to live with it.

- Wherever possible, major decisions should be staged or dramatized.

Case 13: Viewpoint

Al Bello is a paid United Fund leader. Jessica James is the owner of her own business. They are good friends and frequently get together to discuss their successes and failures. "I've been agonizing over my decisions for over twenty years," claims Al Bello, "and frankly I believe I should have devoted more time to announcing and articulating my decisions and less time to making them. I believe you can make a so-so decision and, providing you announce it with decisiveness, conviction, and strength, it may accomplish more than a better decision announced in a more routine manner. Does this make sense?"

"I agree," Jessica replies, "that announcing and articulating a decision in a forceful manner is important, but nothing can take away the sting of a bad decision, or even a poor one. Sooner or later the quality of your decisions will catch up to you. My decisions are designed to keep my company in a profit mode so that my employees will continue to work enthusiastically. If I make a decision that disrupts this pattern, I'm in trouble, no matter how much attention and power I put behind the announcement."

"I'm not so sure the quality of one's decisions means that much," states Mr. Bello. "There is a time-lag element. By the time those involved can tell whether a good or bad decision has been made, they have forgotten who made it. Or they don't care. In the future I'm going to make the best possible decision without spending so much time and then spend more time implementing it. If my subordinates think I am a good leader, they will go along with my decisions, good or bad. We should use decisions to communicate our leadership, not our logic."

"I can't follow your rationale on this," Jessica responds. "You are a good leader if you make good decisions. This is true because you are leading in the right direction. The fact that others may not know you are making sound decisions is not as important as your knowing it. And, besides, sooner or later all decisions come back to haunt you. I know."

Which viewpoint would you support? Is there such a thing as a decision time lag? Do we hold our leaders responsible for their decisions? Is the decision-making process overestimated as a leadership essential? (The author's comments are given in the back of the book.)

Case 14: Decision

Members of the board of trustees for a small, private foundation are writing the criteria for the selection of a new president. The previous president left the organization in a shambles because of a series of poor decisions.

Three board members agree that it would be a good idea for anyone submitting an application to also submit a decision-making track record. The record would include a list of major decisions over the past five years, the applicant's assessment of why they were good decisions, and verification from a responsible party that the decisions turned out well for all concerned. Anyone who does not submit such a record will not be considered.

The remaining two trustees take an opposing view. They believe it is impossible to verify whether a decision is good or bad, that many highly qualified leaders would not submit applications because of this requirement, and that it is virtually impossible to determine ahead of time the decision-making capabilities of an applicant.

Which group would you support? What suggestion might you make to help them select a good decision maker without having each applicant submit a record? Do you feel the board is placing too much emphasis on decision making to the detriment of more important characteristics? (Turn to the back of the book to read the author's opinion.)

Mark each statement True or False.

Self-Test

_____ 1. Improving your decision-making ability is a good way to put more leadership into your style.

_____ 2. The way you announce and articulate a decision has little to do with the leadership image you communicate.

_____ 3. Subordinates keep accurate records of the decisions their leaders make.

_____ 4. Good decision makers always follow the same logical, pre-scribed procedure.

_____ 5. It is best to acknowledge bad decisions and make immediate corrections.

_____ 6. Following a standard decision-making process for thirty days can improve the quality of decisions for the inexperienced leader.

_____ 7. The group process invariably produces better and faster decisions.

_____ 8. A poor decision, made with decisiveness, can be better than no decision at all.

_____ 9. Decision making does not bother leaders as much as followers.

_____ 10. There is no such thing as a "gut decision."

Turn to the back of the book to check your answers.

TOTAL CORRECT _____

Be a Visionary!

It is a time for a new
generation of leadership to
cope with new problems
and new opportunities.
For there is a new world
to be won.

John Fitzgerald Kennedy

Leaders Create and Articulate a Mission to Their Followers

Being a star communicator! Providing followers with the right rewards! Developing a balanced power package! Making decisive decisions! All are part of the leadership star model. But in addition to all this, leaders must furnish direction. They must lead toward something of meaning and significance. A potential victory must be provided somewhere down the road.

On a flight to Washington, D.C., I sat next to a young Native American who was flying to the capital to accept a Small Business Administration award for starting a successful business to recycle steel slag. We touched on many subjects, but I was most impressed with how he interpreted the mission of his small company. "Our purpose is to live in harmony with the land—to use what we take, to return what we do not need. It is the Indian way." The goal of his company was to make money and survive; its mission was conservation of natural resources, and he knew exactly how to articulate it.

Peter Drucker, in his book *Managing for Results,** discusses the importance of a single organization goal for managers and employees. If such a goal exists (and is articulated), it could and should be converted into a mission. A mission has two purposes: It gives the whole organization (managers and employees alike) a sense of unity and purpose, and it keeps everyone moving with enthusiasm in the right direction.

NEED FOR A BIGGER VISION

Most people underestimate their need (and that of others) to have a high vision or dream on the horizon. The majority of managers fall into this category. So do some leaders. That is the reason many organizations falter. It is also the reason why work is nothing but *work* for most people.

Sad though it is to acknowledge, individual productivity in America (taking into consideration technological conditions at the time) was never greater than during World War II. Why? Because almost everybody had a mission. They wanted to be part of a victory that was over the horizon. Of course, peacetime missions may be less inspirational, but the possibility of inspiration exists in all situations where people operate as a group.

True leaders acknowledge with enthusiasm that humankind does not live or work for bread alone (neither dollars nor subsistence). They know that employees want something beyond dollars, benefits, security, promotions, recognition, and the promise of retirement. They want to be a part of something bigger than themselves—and the key word is *part*. Workers become followers when they become part of an effort that has significance. They feel differently when they are part of a movement or

*New York, Harper & Row, 1964.

team. It is not just little personal victories that most employees seek; rather, they want to participate and share in a group victory.

A visionary is one whose ideas and plans are not always practical. A goal setter is one who makes practical goals exciting and reachable. Perhaps what is needed is a combination of the two—a leader who can articulate a vision or dream and back it up with small, reachable goals that, once achieved, provide victories along the way. Whether the vision ever materializes may not be important, as long as it provides direction and supplements the motivation to reach the goals.

A VISIONARY VS. A GOAL SETTER

A mission can be a rainbow in the sky; a goal can be a chore. A mission can be a dream or a vision; a goal a duty one is expected to perform. A mission provides meaning and self-fulfillment; a goal provides rewards that are soon forgotten. Generally, a goal is more immediate, more pragmatic, and more mundane than a mission.

A goal, by definition, must be reachable; a mission need not. A mission does not have to be accomplished—and may never be. But it must stir the imagination and feed the soul.

Many people complain that they do not feel good about the work they are doing. There is little personal gratification, little recognition, little glory. Perhaps it is because their leaders have not provided a sense of mission that would give their efforts meaning. The leader who can create and articulate such a mission will always have followers.

Two entrepreneurs started similar businesses at the same time under similar conditions. The goal of the first entrepreneur was to show a profit after two years and then double it annually for the following three years. The goal of the second entrepreneur was to create a model or prototype business that would attract national attention and, as a result, could be franchised across the country. Those in the "start-up operation" would be furnished key franchise opportunities (at minimum cost) ahead of outsiders.

Although both entrepreneurs had a goal, number two also had a vision. He or she could picture a model operation that was so good others would want to copy it, and soon it would be copied throughout the country. The difference is significant. Perhaps number one wanted to be a profitable owner/manager, whereas number two wanted to be a leader in the industry.

A successful developer/builder conceived of a retirement center that would be a showcase for the region. The center would be elegant but affordable, safe and secure, close to community activities, functional but not crowded. He and a staff of architects spent three years on the design. Once the property was acquired, the builder conducted a series of meetings for staff, subcontractors, community leaders, and others concerned with the development. At each meeting he painted a vision. Then, through other forms of communication, he kept the dream alive while the center developed, step by step. Once it was completed, everyone was amazed at the high level of productivity achieved both by paid construction people and volunteers.

Although not true in all cases, managers are apt to settle for immediate productivity goals, without creating a vision first. Leaders, on the other hand, are apt to start with an exciting, imaginative vision to capture minds and enthusiasm, then supplement the dream with immediate goals. Leaders appeal to pride and fulfillment; they attempt to make followers feel important by providing them with the opportunity to share in a victory that is bigger than themselves.

LEADERS SUPPORT THE NEED FOR MISSION

The topmost point in the leadership star (Formula) represents the need for a vision or mission, as the leaders in the original survey insisted. Although a few preferred the term *overriding purpose,* all were enthusiastic about the need to have and articulate something beyond typical goals. To some, providing a mission is the essence of leadership.

There was also agreement that creating the right mission and then articulating it is a major challenge. Their comments are a measure of both their enthusiasm for the idea and their struggles to make it work:

"Any leadership concept that does not include the responsibility of creating an overall purpose or vision is shallow indeed."

"The purpose of a mission is to provide direction, and direction is what leadership is all about."

"I agree with the mission idea, but it is easier for a minister or a politician to produce one than the head of a business organization."

"The most important thing a mission does is motivate the leader."

CONVERTING A PRIMARY GOAL INTO A MISSION

Sometimes a goal can be converted into a mission by following a procedure like this: (1) Isolate the three most important goals within the group or organization; (2) select the one that has the greatest appeal; (3) convert this goal into a mission by giving it a new, dynamic title; and (4) articulate it in such a way that it stands above organizational goals.

Another way to come up with a suitable mission is through the technique of brainstorming. The leader calls some members of the group together and says, "What are we really trying to do here?" Often a mission will surface in the first session. The group technique makes sense because those who will carry out the mission should, if possible, be involved in creating it. If it doesn't stir their imaginations or give them a sense of pride, it is probably the wrong mission for that group. Of course, it is also important that the leader be committed to the mission. A good mission is often an extension of the leader—an integral part of his or her positive force.

WINNING IS AN ACCEPTABLE MISSION

It is not always possible for a leader to create an ideal or original mission. But even if a leader can't create one that inspires or excites, all is not lost. The sense of pride that accompanies winning can be a good mission. Many times there is no need to look further. In this respect, coaches have a big advantage over other leaders. They have an inherent, automatic mission—winning! And best of all, every time they start a new season their sense of mission is renewed.

Winning is upbeat, exciting, and full of personal rewards. If you have ever participated in a sport, you may know the pride that comes from playing on a winning team. There is nothing quite like it. But teams are not the only organizations that win. It is a great feeling to be with a business organization that is making a profit and expanding (winning). It is a great feeling to work for an educational institution that has high standards and successful programs (winning); it is a great feeling to be on a police force that is admired and respected by the community it serves (winning).

Any type or size of organization or group can be a winner.

TEST YOUR MISSION-WRITING CAPABILITIES

On the following page you will find two opportunities to test your capacity to write mission statements and, perhaps, design a mission for an operation that needs one. You need not occupy a management or leadership role to complete these exercises.

ARTICULATION

Many leaders forget that it is as important to articulate a mission as to create one. They assume that if the mission is a good one it will survive on its own. They are wrong. A mission, to be successful, must be transmitted clearly and frequently through all available communication networks. If a mission can be encapsulated in a slogan or catchphrase, it is more likely to be remembered.

If the leader communicates the mission, it will have greater impact. He or she should, without question, make communicating the mission the number-one priority in all talks to members of the group, either personally or on video tape. The more a mission is personalized by the top leader the better.

A few political pundits believe that President Reagan did not win the national election in 1980 because his mission was more acceptable

---

Writing Mission Statements

Leaders who create their own missions are usually enthusiastic about them. And if a mission can be encapsulated in a slogan, or mission statement, it is easier to communicate. With these two factors in mind, you are invited to try your hand at creating a mission statement for the following situations. When you are finished, you might enjoy comparing your statements with those of your fellow students (if you are part of a seminar or class).

You are the director of fund raising for a private college. Your goal is to raise $10 million, a 20 percent jump over last year. Write a mission statement in the space below.

_____

_____

You are a high school coach. Your goal is to be conference champion. Write a mission statement that will contribute to your goal.

_____

_____

As corporate president, you are seeking a mission statement that will improve the image of your organization as well as contribute to higher profits. Write your best effort below.

_____

_____

---

than Carter's to the majority of American people; he won because he did a superior job of articulating it. From the day he left the governorship of California to the day he won the election, Reagan accepted speaking engagements in every part of the United States. Not only did his mission (to return to a more conservative America) capture his audiences, it became more and more motivating to the future President himself.

Some observers believe that the success of a mission depends more on articulation (90 percent) than on content (10 percent). They are quick to point out, for example, that making a profit is the true mission of any business enterprise. Yet this mission is never fully articulated. Workers are not reminded that if their firm does not win in the marketplace, their jobs are in jeopardy; that if the firm cannot make money, there will be no capital for growth, which in turn create more opportunities. As a mission statement, "make a profit" is probably inspiring only to those who benefit directly—stockholders and employees who participate in profit-sharing plans. But put another way, the profit motive can inspire all: "Keep your chin up, you're with a winner," or "When the company makes a profit, we all win." These are the kind of positive statements workers like to hear.

It is the responsibility of all leaders to lead the group in the direction that will provide the greatest benefit for all. But the meaning of both *benefit* and *direction* must be understood by the group. If not, group members may follow another course. It is only when leaders constantly communicate where they are going, why they are going there, and what it will mean when they arrive that they are fulfilling their leadership potential.

Leaders who abdicate the opportunity to establish and articulate a mission are letting both themselves and their followers down. They are backing away from the heart of leadership.

Finding a Mission

Please write a mission statement for a group project of your own, then answer the questions. If you have eight or more yes answers, it would appear you have designed a suitable mission for your group.

Mission: _____

		Yes	No
1.	Does this mission lead everyone in the group in the best possible direction?	☐	☐
2.	Will it benefit all members equally?	☐	☐
3.	Will it help to sustain and protect the organization over the long term?	☐	☐
4.	Can I, as a leader, articulate the mission clearly to all members of the group?	☐	☐
5.	Can the mission be expressed as a slogan?	☐	☐
6.	Will the members of my group accept the mission with enthusiasm?	☐	☐
7.	Am I highly enthusiastic about it myself?	☐	☐
8.	Will the mission increase motivation appreciably?	☐	☐
9.	Is is sufficiently visionary to work?	☐	☐
10.	Is it the best mission under the circumstances?	☐	☐

**MISSIONS AND
POSITIVE FORCE**

As the Formula graphic illustrates, a winning mission becomes an extension of the positive force communicated by the leader. Although some good missions are the result of group consensus (recommended), leaders must often create their own missions, without help. After all, leaders have the view from the top—the advantage of perspective.

In using their talents to come up with a mission, leaders must recognize that each group or organization—business, educational, government, religious, community—should create its own special mission. To copy the mission of another group is to miss the point. And a mission should always have the personal stamp of the leader. It should grow out of, and reflect, his or her positive force.

Superior leaders find much of their motivation from the very missions they develop. Missions are, therefore, self-serving. They can, and often do, motivate the leader more than the followers.

Not a bad endorsement.

SUMMARY

• A mission is more than a goal. It reflects the overriding purpose of the organization or institution. It should inspire both leaders and followers.

• A mission has three purposes: to motivate followers, to hold a group together, and to head it in the right direction.

• Sometimes a primary organization goal can be converted into a mission.

• Articulating a mission can be as important as the mission itself.

• Practical, short-term productivity goals can be effective when tied to an overriding mission.

• A mission (more than the other four points in the star) should be an extension of the positive force created by the leader.

Professor Robinson is a master teacher. His course on Leadership is extremely popular. Maria, an office manager at twenty-six, is one of his assertive students. After a lecture on the importance of mission to the leadership concept, Maria volunteered this comment:

"I can understand why top leaders need to create a mission to motivate subordinates and to keep the organization alive and moving in the right direction, but I think it should stop there. Those of us at the bottom who run small departments should spend our time carrying out the big missions sent down to us. Creating one of our own is a joke."

Professor Robinson answered: "Does this mean that as an office manager you could not benefit from a tailor-made mission for just your employees? Isn't it possible that you could accept the company mission and at the same time create a smaller, but still effective, one of your own? What I'm leading up to is this. Sometimes, a departmental mission will do more to create team spirit than a corporate mission handed down from above. You could try to be the most efficient department, most envied, or most friendly. If you succeeded, it would give the department an identity, and members would feel they belonged to a winner."

Maria replied: "Everyone in our outfit is goal-happy. I get so many goals handed down to me, I don't have time to develop any special mission. It would just be another responsibility. Besides, my employees are too sophisticated—they'd just laugh at the idea."

Professor Robinson continued: "I believe that creating a mission might be highly motivating to you, Maria. You might be more enthusiastic about a little mission you created yourself than a big one that trickled down from above. I'm not so sure that a mission at the bottom of an organization is not a good idea. It might make as much sense as one from the top. And it might contribute to productivity more."

Assume that you are a member of the class and Professor Robinson calls on you for your opinion. How would you reply? Would you support Maria or the professor? (The author's opinion is given in the back of the book.)

Case 16: Involvement

Ramon Garcia, a hospital administrator, developed a mission statement for the 140-bed facility he supervises: "Better care—lower prices." Mr. Garcia tried out his mission statement on both internal and community groups. It was a great success. He then suggested to Louise Loring, his director of Human Resources, that she ask all hospital managers to develop a mission statement of their own. Mr. Garcia was careful to explain that departmental missions should follow the general mission in theme and certainly not conflict with it.

Mrs. Loring is a believer in participatory management. She quickly called a conference of the sixteen managers representing various medical and nonmedical services. In presenting the idea she pointed out that establishing and maintaining a mission is a demonstration of good leadership. She also got the group to agree on the following: (1) Missions shall be expressed as short statements. (2) They must be accepted by the majority of departmental personnel. (3) They must be submitted within fifteen days. (4) All slogans will be posted in a public place so that everyone will know the mission of each department. (5) A winner will be selected, and those in the winning department will receive an extra day off with pay.

How would you evaluate this approach? Do you think it will be successful? What changes would you make? (See the back of the book for the author's suggestions.)

Mark the statements True or False.

_____ 1. A goal and a mission are the same thing.

_____ 2. There is little relationship between a mission and a positive force.

_____ 3. Peter Drucker states that all organizations can benefit from a single organizational goal, or mission.

_____ 4. Sometimes having too many goals makes it more difficult to have a single mission.

_____ 5. A vision or mission need not be achieved to be effective.

_____ 6. Winning in itself is not a mission.

_____ 7. It is easier to create a mission than to articulate it.

_____ 8. Goals can never be converted into missions.

_____ 9. Managers are more apt to be visionaries than leaders.

_____ 10. A mission can be an adventure; a goal, a chore.

Turn to the back of the book to check your answers.

TOTAL CORRECT _____

Create a Positive Force

And if the blind lead the
blind, both shall fall into
the ditch.

Matthew 15:14

Successful Leaders Generate Waves of Activity

Drawing upon all power sources, especially personality power, a leader creates and maintains a positive force that pulls followers in one direction with enthusiasm and dedication. Nothing is ever dull or routine in the presence of a true leader. Things are always jumping! This physical, psychological, and spiritual force constitutes the heart of our strategic model (star).

In creating this intensity of power, the leader must make maximum use of his or her communication system, see that followers receive proper rewards, make decisive decisions, and keep the mission in focus. Not an easy combination! Although all points in the star are equally important and interrelated, the energy that keeps them functioning at optimal level emanates from the center. It is this leadership power that energizes and illuminates the star. Like any power system (generator, battery storing an electrical charge, etc.), the central force keeps the communication network alive, provides the vehicles to deliver rewards, creates good decisions, and, drawing heavily from role and personality and knowledge power sources, leads the organization to high productivity and success. And all of this in the direction of a preestablished mission!

> Mary started her first season as a girls' soccer coach very naive, nervous, and with little hope of success. Only a few girls had turned out, and they were an undisciplined bunch. Her heart sank as she watched the first day's practice.
>
> But Mary was determined that things would improve. Because of her positive attitude, she soon built a happy relationship with each player. The girls began to have fun at practice, and after winning a few games they started building skill, confidence, and poise. When Mary told her fellow high school coaches that she intended to win the conference title, they laughed. But when the season was over, her team had the trophy to prove it.
>
> Mary is no ordinary coach. She knows that most leaders have many enviable characteristics: most are intelligent, perceptive, personable, self-motivating, and courageous. She doesn't downplay these traits, but she knows that there is one other critical trait that most people never think of when describing leadership.
>
> *It is the ability to create a positive force.*
>
> In contrast to the other coaches, Mary had created, communicated, and maintained a consistent positive force. Her girls, without knowing it, were caught up in something that made them reach beyond their everyday potential as competitors. It was this force that had made the difference in their season.

WHAT IS A POSITIVE FORCE?

In one sense, it is nothing more than positive expectations. But, in another sense, it is a dynamic force that emanates from a leader and pulls the entire group into an inner circle of involvement and activity. Once it gets started, it seems to generate vigor and confidence. It stirs people up. It motivates. It removes obstacles. It leads to constructive action. It is, in effect, a form of energy. It gets people on the right track and keeps them moving. It stems from the positive attitude of the leader, but it manifests itself in action. Once a positive force gets under way, a group psychology takes over. Like a cyclone or tornado, it picks up momentum. Although it seems to feed on itself, the increased velocity comes from the dynamics (contributions) of the members of the group. It is difficult to stand on the sidelines and not be drawn into it.

When there is an absence of positive, forceful leadership, lethargy takes over. The sensation of motion disappears. Lassitude prevails. The organization or group becomes sluggish and fat. In reference to the Leadership Formula, the tips of the star begin to sag, the star begins to shrink, and the luster disappears. When this occurs, followers are left uninspired and, ultimately, disenchanted.

When leadership does not generate a consistent positive force, those required to exist inside organizational frameworks usually relax, mark time, and take the course of least resistance. Nothing separates a manager from a leader more than being able to create and maintain a positive force. Managers can often survive through controls, efficiency, and "good management" of an operation. A leader must be sufficiently dynamic to create a force that will carry the organization to new heights.

HOW DO YOU CREATE A POSITIVE FORCE?

Leaders create the force in their individual ways. They glamorize their role positions, making them the center of action. They turn their personality power loose, sending rays of energy in all directions. They show personal vigor; they demonstrate a bearing that communicates strength. They create the feeling that something good is about to happen.

Like a pebble dropped into a quiet pool, the power of your positive attitude starts the force, but it is your special characteristics that push it into wider and wider circles. Each leader must develop his or her own centrifugal-power configuration, employing all positive personality characteristics and elements to keep the force alive.

But it all starts with a positive attitude.

Remaining positive under trying conditions is not an easy task. Yet, if you wish to be a successful leader, you have no choice. You must remain positive because your positive attitude is the source of the power. Your positive attitude communicates to those you lead that they are headed in the right direction, that there are exciting goals within reach, that something better lies over the horizon. A positive attitude in a leader builds positive expectations in the minds of the group, whereas a negative attitude destroys them. When a leader turns negative, the positive force dissipates as quickly as the air in a punctured balloon.

AS A LEADER YOU ARE ALWAYS ON CENTER STAGE

Because leaders transmit much of their positive force through their presence or personality, they must always put their best foot forward. They must always be in charge. They must always be "up" so that their followers will never feel "down."

"I can let my negative feelings show to my secretary and immediate staff, but never to my employees."

"You can never let down in front of the troops."

"When I'm not up, neither is the team."

"Leadership and being positive are inseparable."

"I need the weekend on the ranch so I can come back Monday and be positive again."

Being constantly on stage can make or break a leader, especially in the world of politics, where the pressure is intense. But this kind of visibility also is important for coaches, corporate leaders, youth workers, ministers, and many others in leadership roles. Whatever your leadership position may be, now or in the future, this responsibility will have more meaning to you after you complete the "Press Conference" exercise on the next page.

PERSONALITY AND VOICE POWER

Personality power plays a leading role in the development of a positive force. When I interviewed leaders, their body language told me immediately that they were take-charge people. I could feel the force of their personalities as I entered their offices. In fact, at times it seemed as if I had walked into a magnetic field.

Their grooming, diction, and bearing communicated personal power, but, looking back, I was most impressed by their voices. The tone and the manner in which they talked communicated a positive force. I could tell they were deliberately using their voices to impress me with their leadership strength. It worked because, to a measurable degree, personality power is voice power and, again to a measurable degree, positive force begins with the voice of the leader.

PERSONAL ACTIVITY CONTRIBUTES TO A POSITIVE FORCE

Successful leaders are always on the move. They transfer their positive attitudes into physical action. They create a flurry of activity that has a domino effect. It sets the tempo for others to follow.

Leaders operate in the sea of activity they themselves create and then watch it flow throughout their organization. This is the way one executive secretary describes her boss, a recognized leader:

Press Conference

To establish yourself as a positive force, you must communicate the impression that you are in charge whenever you are in the presence of others. To help yourself learn to do this, assume you are the subject of a televised press conference. All eyes are on you as you walk into the studio.

List in order of priority the impressions you would like to project to your audience, placing (in the left column) number 1 next to the characteristic you feel most important, and so on down the line. In the right-hand column, rank in order of priority the characteristics you need to work on the most.

Priority		*Work Needed*
_____	imperturbability	_____
_____	positive attitude	_____
_____	vigor	_____
_____	positive bearing	_____
_____	friendliness	_____
_____	excellent speaking ability	_____
_____	good grammar and diction	_____
_____	knowledge	_____
_____	sincerity-honesty	_____
_____	sense of humor	_____
_____	good grooming	_____
_____	decisiveness	_____

Now match your numbers against each category. If you discover that you have entered a low number (high priority) on both sides of a factor, any improvement you make in this area will pay double dividends in creating a stronger in-charge impression.

"The only time you will find things peaceful around here is when she is on a trip. She thrives on activity, and it's catching. I sometimes feel I'm in the center of a hurricane. Everyone here at the home office knows immediately when she is back from a trip. In fact, we feel the storm coming ahead of time."

MOTIVATIONAL DELEGATING

There are two kinds of delegating. One form is designed to get work done—to meet production schedules and so on. In the other form, motivational delegating, leaders assign research, ask for reports, and seek advice. They constantly keep people involved by giving them something new to do to keep them from getting bored. Motivational delegating helps people reach their potential. Not that the tasks delegated do not need to be accomplished. Most of them do. The idea is that they keep people moving, creating and releasing their talent and energy. This kind of delegating enhances the positive force that is already alive. It keeps life in the group or organization. Leaders seem to sense that this kind of delegating is an extension of their personal force.

"I motivate my people almost 100 percent through delegation. I cook up ideas that can't help but have a positive thrust—and then I turn them over to others. I never want anyone on my staff ever to catch up and relax. They wouldn't be happy if this occurred."

"It's my responsibility as a leader to keep everyone moving, living at their capacity, contributing. I hate boredom myself, and it really galls me to see my people idle. So if they don't have enough to do, I create it."

"Inactivity always leads to trouble. I do not want my employees to live in a stressful climate, but I want them busy at all times. I will resort to anything in the book to make this happen."

It is obvious that coaches cannot merely wait for their teams to catch fire; executives cannot sit back and wait for their employees to energize themselves; ministers cannot expect their congregations to provide their own spiritual guidance; and community leaders cannot expect volunteers to motivate themselves. Leaders must step in and make these things happen. Motivational delegating is the prime tool in their kits.

MAINTAINING MOMENTUM THROUGH A COMMUNICATION NETWORK

Once created, how can the positive force be kept alive? Once there is movement, how can it be maintained?

The answer is communication.

Without good communication, a positive force cannot get started, let alone thrive. The leader must set and maintain an effective organizational

Contract Exercise

(Become a More Positive Force by Making a Contract with Yourself.)

It is possible to become a more positive force in any leadership role—as a parent or a community volunteer. In this exercise, you make a contract with yourself to demonstrate you can be a more positive force in the future. This means you will need to increase your enthusiasm and communicate a more positive posture and attitude. The recommended procedure is as follows.

Step 1. Find a suitable observer—someone who sees you in operation on a daily basis: your boss, a colleague, a mentor, a friend, or family member. Make sure it is a person you respect, who is familiar with your behavior patterns.

Step 2. Take this person to lunch or dinner and explain that you have made a contract with yourself to extend your positive influence into wider circles. You are sincere in your desire to improve your leadership style. The reason for a structured meeting is to make certain the contract is not interpreted as a temporary or offhand decision.

Step 3. At the meeting, ask the individual if he or she will observe the way you behave during a thirty-day period. Ask them to tell you at the end of this period if they can sense any behavior modifications that indicate you are acting in a more positive manner. They can make mental or written notes during the period, but should not talk to you about the experiment or tell anyone else about it.

Step 5. At the end of the thirty-day period, set up a second meeting to discuss results. Were behavior changes noticeable? Did others, not involved in the experiment, notice? Were all changes an improvement? What can be done to keep the positive force alive in the future?

Step 6. Evaluate the observer's comments and make a long-term contract for continued improvement.

communication network. Without it, the positive force will die in the leader's office.

A communication network keeps a leader in touch with the people he or she leads. It can include every kind of medium—from a personal note to a slick house organ, from a telephone call to a nationally televised public affairs program. A network is a media system that allows members of a group to be in on the action and leaders to keep in touch with the feelings of the group when personal contact is impossible. A good network can keep everyone in tune with organizational goals. Members of the group know where they are, why they are doing what they are doing, and what may happen down the road. They feel they belong.

THE FORMAL COMMUNICATION NETWORK

Every organization, large or small, has its formal communication system. The following case illustrates how extensive such a system can be.

Peter Gomez is the newly hired president of the XYZ corporation. XYZ used a headhunting firm to find its new leader because the poor performance of its previous president convinced the board the firm needed proven talent. A new, fresh, positive force might put some life back into the firm. When Mr. Gomez arrived, his first priority was to analyze the communication network. Total revamping was called for. Within thirty days, Mr. Gomez (1) replaced the communications officer; (2) set up a series of meetings; (3) wrote the lead article for the next issue of the house publication; (4) purchased video equipment for the training department and prepared six tapes to be shown to all employees; (5) scheduled a tour every week to inspect all eleven departments in the organization; (6) initiated a weekly bulletin outlining key developments of the past week, to be distributed to all employees, every Monday morning; (7) set aside every Friday afternoon from 3 to 5 for informal chats with employees; (8) asked his new communications officer to restyle the house publication; (9) increased the communications budget.

Although Mr. Gomez knew that he would not be able to maintain such a flurry of activity over a sustained period, he decided it was necessary to launch a positive force that would eventually turn the organization around. Without a new, revised communication network, this could not be accomplished.

One way to perceive both the importance and difficulty of creating a positive force is to measure your own reaction to your manager or leader. Please ask yourself these questions:

• Are you, as a subordinate or observer, caught up in the positive force created by this leader? Can you sense its presence?

• Has this leader created a dynamic, positive group acceptance of his or her leadership, to the point that members of the group are totally motivated to follow?

• Is this leader aware that he or she is constantly on stage, or is this leader sometimes negative or apathetic?

• Do you, under this leader, feel you are going somewhere? Is the organization moving? Is there an upbeat feeling in the group?

• Would you be willing to follow this leader in the face of strong opposition from others?

• Does this leader make it easy for you to stay positive?

Tough questions—yet they get to the essence of what leadership is all about. So whatever leadership role you occupy or will assume in the future, you must, if you wish to be successful over the long term, accept the challenge of becoming a positive force. How powerful a force must you create, and how will you know it is adequate?

Just turn around. If your followers are following, all is well!

A positive force (along with other parts of the Formula) is the essence of leadership.

SUMMARY

- You cannot exist as a leader without developing a positive force that will inspire those who follow you.

- A positive force generates constructive action.

- A positive force stems from a positive attitude, which is at the heart of your personality power.

- Leaders need to show great energy.

- As a leader, you are always on center stage.

- A good communication system permits the leader of a large organization to communicate his or her positive force to all members of the group, no matter how far away they may be.

Case 17: Charisma

Justine and Rebecca have been good friends since college days, when both prepared for careers in youth work. Justine is currently director of a YMCA in northern California. Rebecca is a Girl Scout executive for a large council in southern California. Both are attending a leadership seminar sponsored by a nationally known foundation. They are sitting around the dinner table discussing the importance of creating and maintaining a positive force. Justine comments:

"My observation tells me that charisma is the primary source of a positive force. This is especially true in youth activities, because kids are so impressionable. If kids are to respond, there has to be a touch of magic in the leader's personality—a something that makes the leader a model. Without this, it's impossible for leaders to establish themselves as a moving force."

"You say that," replies Rebecca, "because you are long on charisma, and you rely on it. What about plain Janes like me? Can we never be leaders just because we are not blessed with charisma? I believe we can lead if we develop good, positive attitudes. That is what young people want in a leader. Someone who looks at the good side and transmits confidence. Attitude is the answer, not charisma."

Do you support Justine or Rebecca? Why? Could you build a case that a positive attitude is a charismatic characteristic? (The author's opinion is given in the back of the book.)

Fred Fisher, executive vice-president of a large utility, and Jane Grey, public relations officer for the same firm, are having lunch in the executive dining room.

"I agree with the positive force idea," states Fred, "and we are fortunate to have J. B. as our president. He really stays positive, moves around, and somehow provides us with the vision and force we need to keep growing. He is a remarkable leader and certainly makes my job easier."

"In a way that is true," replied Jane, "but the positive force he represents still needs to be communicated to our nine thousand employees, our stockholders, and customers. He cannot do this alone. In fact, it is about 10 percent effort on his part and 90 percent effort on our part. I agree he has a good image for us to transmit, but we still have to do it. He still needs to be sold in every publication, on television, and in all media. You might say he creates a positive force, but we communicate it."

"You may be overstating your own importance. I believe the lowest employee we have would feel the positive force he creates without any formal communications. A positive force is personality based, and it transmits itself more through the grapevine and personal contact than through the media. One employee catches it and passes it on to another. You're saying, in effect, that you manufacture the positive force that keeps this company moving."

"No, I'm saying that without a well-organized formal communication system, any positive force created by the top leader would eventually die on the vine. J. B. couldn't get his positive force beyond you and his personal staff without us. We enhance, maintain, and protect his image. We keep the force going."

"I'm not saying we should eliminate the PR department," said Fred, "but you totally underestimate how much J. B. does on his own."

Does Ms. Grey overstate her case? Does Mr. Fisher underestimate the importance of formal communications? Take a position on the problem and defend it. (The author's reaction is given in the back of the book.)

Case 18: Communications

Self-Test

Mark each statement True or False.

_____ 1. A positive force emanates from a leader and pulls followers into an inner circle of involvement.

_____ 2. Without a positive force created by leaders, the members of a group will take the course of least resistance.

_____ 3. Everyone has the capacity to create a force that people will follow.

_____ 4. A positive attitude is the primary source of a positive force.

_____ 5. It is not advisable for leaders to use their three sources of power to create a positive force.

_____ 6. A positive force transmits itself throughout an organization.

_____ 7. The stronger the positive force, the higher productivity is apt to be.

_____ 8. The fact that "Positive Force" is at the center of the star means that it is more important than the other five foundations.

_____ 9. Leaders, whether they know it or not, are always on center stage.

_____ 10. Nonleaders have the luxury of being negative; leaders do not.

Turn to the back of the book to check your answers.

TOTAL CORRECT _____

Weave More Leadership into Your Management Style

A critic is a man who knows the way but can't drive the car.

Kenneth Tynan

Do It Your Way

Henry and his partner, Jake, are having their regular morning meeting to discuss operational problems in their chain of restaurants. Today the discussion centers on the problem of training mangers.

"Ten years ago," Henry remarks, "we had the time and money to conduct in-house seminars and give our new managers a lot of personal help. Today, with tighter budgets, all we can do is establish the best possible working environment, provide the tools, and hope they will train themselves."

Jake agrees. "If those in our organization who want to be leaders are not self-motivated, there is little we can do to help them."

Henry and Jake have a point.

You could be a national political leader, a corporate executive, a first-line supervisor, a priest, or a community leader. You could also be on the sidelines, a student preparing to be a leader. Whatever your position, if you want to become a better leader and are not self-motivated, you are in trouble. That is the bad news.

The good news is that if you really want to put more leadership into your style, you can do so. The Formula provides the guidelines, but you must realize it is a do-it-yourself project.

How you go about weaving the Leadership Formula into your style will depend upon your experience and the role you occupy.

THE LEADERSHIP STAR AS A MODEL

If one accepts the Leadership Formula (star) as a model that communicates some of the essence of leadership, it can act as a reference point for personal growth. For example, college graduates could retain the Formula in their minds and let it guide them as they grow into management and leadership roles. They could use it to balance management with leadership skills, for self-evaluation when progress is slow, to keep their dreams and aspirations alive. The star can and should be used as a model for long-term career development.

PINPOINTING WEAK AREAS

For those who occupy management or leadership roles, the Leadership Formula can indicate areas of weakness where immediate improvement would pay big dividends. Although it is possible to show improvement in all six areas, experience indicates that many leaders have neglected (without knowing it) one or two.

Priority Exercise

Once people become acquainted with all six fundamentals in the Formula (the five points and center of the star), they sense where their greatest weakness lies. In this exercise, please give top priority to that area where improvement will do most for your leadership image (place "1" in the appropriate square). Then place numbers 2, 3, 4, 5, and 6 in the remaining squares, in the order you perceive self-improvement is needed. In doing this, you set the order in which you intend to weave more leadership into your management style.

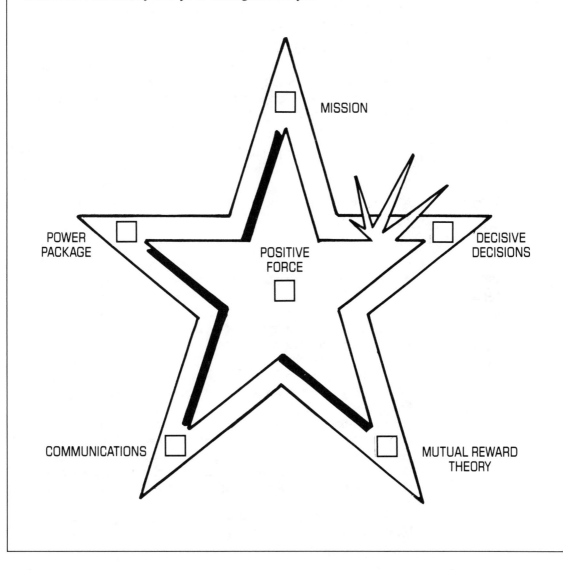

When, as the result of a seminar, John took a look at the Leadership Formula, he became aware that he had lost his punch as a positive force and, as a result, his leadership had become less effective in the other five areas. After the seminar, John reactivated himself as a dynamic force and was, once again, on the move.

Attending the same seminar, Anne became aware that she had not provided her followers with a mission to which they could tie their immediate goals. After the seminar, she did some serious rethinking about the direction her organization was taking. At her next staff meeting, Anne articulated a new mission that not only motivated her group but gave her more enthusiasm.

It took the seminar and the Leadership Formula to convince Jake that he had not developed or adequately used his power package. As a result, he returned to his leadership role with more confidence and renewed determination to become a leader/manager instead of simply a manager.

Everyone, of course, interprets the Formula (star) differently. And everyone decides how and when they may or may not weave all or part of it into their behavioral pattern. Experience shows that most leaders who are exposed to the formula for the first time discover at least one weakness that they decide to strengthen.

RATING OTHERS AS WELL AS YOURSELF

Another advantage of the model is being able to use the essence of leadership (the six foundations) to evaluate the leadership effectiveness of others. Comparing one leader against another is especially valuable in the political area. In the appendix is a Leadership Effectiveness Scale for this purpose, which readers can use to rate themselves as well as others. It is of special value when an individual rates himself or herself first, then asks for another's assessment for purposes of comparison. The scale reflects the essence of leadership as communicated in the Leadership Formula.

Should none of the possibilities above fall into your comfort zone, you may decide to use the Formula in your own way. You may, of course, decide that you prefer to remain a manager or a follower. If this is your decision, what you have learned about leadership will help you assess the effectiveness of those who have decided to take the risk. Either way, you come out ahead.

Should you decide to accept the challenge and start enhancing your leadership capabilities, you will want to tread lightly and consider these three suggestions.

Protect Your Flanks.   After a well-known entertainer purchased an expensive fur coat at an exclusive boutique in Las Vegas, she asked to use the telephone to call her insurance agent to make arrangements to have the fur insured immediately. As she hung up the telephone, she remarked to the salesperson, "I need the fur for my image, but I've got to recognize it might be ripped off at any moment."

Leaders have something of the same problem. They must create and maintain an image, but they must accept the fact that some members of the group might, at any time, turn against them. They cannot, unfortunately, purchase insurance for protection, but they must constantly be aware that a disenchanted subordinate might try to undermine them. This, too, goes with the leadership territory.

A good two-way communication network is needed. In addition to transmitting the positive force created by the leader, it must uncover potentially dangerous counterforces so that some form of corrective action can be taken before things get out of hand.

> Mary Mullins, mayor of a community of over fifty thousand residents, was determined to cut down on crime. To this end, she beefed up the resources of the police department. Her efforts paid off handsomely, but other city employees, especially those in the fire department, started to feel neglected and even hostile. Fortunately, Mrs. Mullins received a signal through her communication system that all was not well. She immediately set up a meeting with the fire chief, started to visit outlying stations, and got the local newspaper to run a series of feature articles on the work of the fire department. Her communication system came to her rescue before things got out of hand.

The moment you make the transition to a leadership position, you become a target. You lose the anonymity you enjoyed as a member of the group. You become a topic of conversation around coffee tables, locker rooms, and bars.

As a member of a group, you were comfortable. You had more security, fewer responsibilities, and time to relax and enjoy your colleagues. As a leader, you must try to provide the rewards the members of the group desire, but you have less security yourself. You also have less time and opportunity for casual conversations. Everything suddenly becomes more formal. You find yourself dependent upon your communication systems.

It is easy to see why top political leaders have press agents and public relations specialists to help them create and monitor the positive force that keeps them in office. Even with the assistance they receive, they frequently get into trouble.

If you are a first-line supervisor, a middle manager, a coach, or a volunteer leader, you may not have a staff surrounding you to provide this communication assistance and protection. You may have to do it yourself, thereby discovering that it is far easier to create positive momentum than to keep it going.

Stay In Your Comfort Zone. In becoming a leader, it is important to do it your way. That is, stay within the framework of your own personality. You can become a star communicator, an outstanding decision maker, and a positive force without turning yourself upside down. The idea is to start where you *are* and strengthen yourself in the six leadership areas.

Maintain Your Management Competence. You are encouraged to build your leadership competence on your management skills. This means you must stay current with management developments, along with improving your leadership. Should you neglect your management base, it could undermine your future, even though you have mastered the Leadership Formula and woven the foundations into your style.

With these simple cautions in mind, you are prepared to become the kind of leader/manager or manager/leader you want to be.

Give it your best shot!

SUMMARY

- The primary use for the Leadership Formula (star) is as a model or guide for personal growth.

- The Formula can pinpoint areas of weakness for those already in leadership roles.

- Readers can use the Formula to rate the leadership performance of others.

- Leaders (more than managers) are vulnerable to dissenters.

- Those who desire to become leaders should do so within their own comfort zones or personality frameworks.

- Leaders must maintain their management competence.

Aaron and Rose have been stuck in their management positions for over three years. They agree that the best way to move up is to put more leadership into their style.

Rose plans to do this in a dramatic fashion. Having carefully analyzed her power package, she has decided to work hard on two parts of the Formula and ignore the others.

First, she is going to tighten her discipline line a notch and maintain it with force. She feels it is time to demonstrate her leadership more emphatically. Second, through more group interaction she intends to generate a more positive force within her department. She intends to keep it going by becoming more positive personally, more active, and more assertive in all her dealings with others. She is going to be center stage at all times.

Aaron, more conservative and cautious by nature, feels that each of the foundations is equally important and wishes to achieve balance. He is fearful that if he tightens his authority line without first making sure that his reward system is effective, he might get into trouble. He is also fearful that if he suddenly becomes more of a positive force, the reaction from others might be counterproductive. He intends to gradually upgrade himself in all six areas without calling attention to himself. He feels that this will be most effective in getting him a promotion.

Which strategy do you support? Defend your position. (The author's reactions are given in the back of the book.)

Case 19: Emphasis

Janice is self-confident, capable, and ambitious—a high-energy person. She never does anything halfway; it is all or nothing. Janice switches from one self-improvement project to another at frequent intervals. Everyone envies her energy, enthusiasm, and creativity. Her colleagues have noticed, however, that her follow-through is not always what it should be. There is little structure in her department and her employees are the most undisciplined in the firm.

Jill is also self-confident, capable, and ambitious—and a planner. She goes about everything in a methodical, deliberate manner. Her follow-through is excellent. She shows great attention to detail. Most of her coworkers admire her low-key approach. Some, however, feel she needs to become more of a self-starter and to provide greater recognition to those who work for her.

Both Janice and Jill, after attending a leadership workshop, wish to incorporate the Leadership Formula into their respective styles.

Which, in your opinion, would be most successful? What kind of success would you predict for Janice? Jill? (The author's prediction is in the back of the book.)

Case 20: Prediction

Self-Test

Mark each statement True or False.

_____ 1. Most managers can expect personal help from their superiors in putting more leadership into their style.

_____ 2. Managers are more vulnerable than leaders when it comes to splinter or divisive forces.

_____ 3. Those in nonleadership positions cannot apply any part of the Leadership Formula.

_____ 4. A major personality change is required to weave leadership into one's management style.

_____ 5. One should not attempt to use the Leadership Formula to rate the leadership effectiveness of others.

_____ 6. The Formula (star) is a reference point that communicates the essence of leadership.

_____ 7. It is better to weave one foundation into your style than none at all.

_____ 8. Because all the foundations are interrelated, it can be dangerous to emphasize one at the expense of another.

_____ 9. You can lead managers to the leadership waters but you can't make them drink.

_____ 10. If you are successful in putting more leadership into your style, your superiors and subordinates will notice a positive difference in your behavior.

Turn to the back of the book to check your answers.

TOTAL CORRECT _____

The leadership cases at the end of each chapter were designed to be springboards for individual thinking and discussion purposes. There are no "right" answers to any of them.

At this early stage, all leadership concepts are nebulous. Until more research and experimentation takes place, different points of view should be encouraged.

The following answers, then, are the author's *opinion,* based upon his investigation and interviews. They should serve only as a guide to the independent thinking of the reader and the discussion leader.

Author's Responses to Case Problems

Professor Adams deserves support on the basis that good management practices are essential to good leadership, and nonbusiness professors may not have this important background. The point is well taken, however, that management professors might spend too much time on management and not enough on leadership. Their prejudices might show so much than nonbusiness students might drop the course. You can also build a case that nonmanagement professors might be able to see the total concept more clearly from where they stand. This would put them in the position to introduce experiences and cases of a more general nature.

Leadership courses have been neglected because not enough is known about the subject to provide the basis for a traditional college course. In addition, teachers have not been trained to teach leadership.

CASE 1: CONTROVERSY

Both Elgin and Samantha start from excellent positions. Elgin, with his management expertise, should be able to make a quick and easy transition, providing he can move away from management and concentrate on leadership. Samantha, because of her leadership experiences, may grasp the management skills and fundamentals sooner because she knows they will help her be a better leader. The author, in this case, goes along with Samantha because he senses that Elgin will fight leadership ideas every inch of the way. He will probably be more interested in defending the accepted value of management instead of taking a fresh look at leadership. Samantha, on the other hand, will accept them and weave them into her style without apparent conflict or indecision.

CASE 2: OPINION

From the limited data provided, the author favors Maureen in the short term because she is a strong manager. Gene shows substantial long-term potential, providing he develops his management *and* leadership potential. His high energy level is a signal his leadership potential may be above that of Maureen. Maureen, of course, with her management foundation, can measurably increase productivity through stronger leadership.

CASE 3: HIGH PRODUCER?

CASE 4:
OPPORTUNITY

Leaving Ms. Preston in Operations is easy to defend. It would appear she is a leadership role model as she circulates within the branch system. In this capacity, she would be difficult to replace. Providing Ms. Preston has teaching talents, the idea of having her do in-house leadership training is excellent. Her impact could be extended. If the board makes this decision, the new director of Human Resources should be encouraged to work closely with Ms. Preston so that the leadership gap within the organization can be closed.

CASE 5:
CONFLICT

The author supports the premise that if an individual learns the fundamentals of leadership in one environment, he or she should be able to transfer them to another. If Greg learned and practiced some fundamentals (like those presented in the Formula) in the military, he should have little trouble adapting them to a banking environment. It would appear that Greg is confused between leadership style and fundamentals. He may be having trouble because he is attempting to transfer an authoritative military style to a participatory situation. The fundamentals would fit both styles. As Vicki suggests, if a student learns the leadership basics in the classroom, he or she should be able to take them into any environment.

CASE 6:
POTENTIAL

The author, naturally, gives his support to Jim. Bob seems to feel he must take his winning style completely apart and rebuild it to incorporate the fundamentals. This is not the case. Bob can weave one or more fundamentals into his style without disrupting it. As he does this, it may be necessary to make minor adjustments and modifications, but that is as far as it need go. He will, however, improve and strengthen his present style because he will fill in the weak spots in his previous emphasis on fundamentals. Put another way, his effective style will improve because it will be based upon a stronger foundation. When Bob senses the difference between style and substance, his fears should dissipate.

CASE 7:
IMPROVEMENT

A formal course in public speaking would probably provide Ms. Blake with the most help, if she took the course seriously, became involved, and stayed with it to the end. Additional live-audience experiences and practice with her video equipment would also help. It would also be beneficial for Ms. Blake to study other speakers and improve her skills through comparative analysis.

CASE 8:
ENHANCEMENT

Both Regina and Matthew should go for an MBA, but augment the program with one or more demanding communication courses. If possible, they should find an MBA program that either includes pure communication courses or will permit substitutes.

Ministers and all other religious leaders who incorporate MRT into their style will automatically strengthen their leadership because they will have better contact with their congregations and a better knowledge of their members' religious and nonreligious needs. Ralph's compassion for others should make the adoption and application of MRT easy and more effective. Still, it is doubtful that this will happen, because he is not enthusiastic about it. Perhaps he does not sense a need to be a stronger leader or build better relationships with his congregation. He seems to be satisfied with things as they are. Unless he comes to the realization that MRT could help him serve God better, nothing will happen.

CASE 9: COMPASSION

The best way to convince oneself of the value of MRT is to actually use it and measure the results. Chances are therefore good that after Mr. Nelson and Mr. Castelletti work out a better reward system between themselves, Mr. Castelletti will become more enthusiastic. Mr. Castelletti's fear is understandable but not justified. It is a comfortable approach to improving relationships and can be used in any environment with any style. Mr. Castelletti needs to be convinced that it will work as well for him, using his own approach and his own words, and that it is not just a technique for psychologists. Receiving the right rewards is as important to truckers as anyone else.

CASE 10: FEAR

Gloria may be a little optimistic about her chances of turning Jane into a forceful leader, but it is a real possibility. Assertiveness training seminars in recent years have demonstrated this can happen. Nobody is born to be either a follower or a leader. In this area one can be what one wants to be. This is not to say that *anyone* can become President of the United States, but it does say that anyone who wants to be a local PTA or church leader can become one. Jane, with Gloria's help, can develop the courage to stand up to others. She can learn to apply structure. The very fact that Gloria sees Jane in the role as her assistant is an indication that the potential is there.

CASE 11: COURAGE

Captain Small builds an excellent case that MRT and structure are not only compatible but mutually dependent. One works much better when the other is present. This is perhaps even more true in the military than in less structured environments. In short, the more structure required, the more MRT is needed. Any military officer who can build a disciplined fighting unit on a sound human relations platform is going to be a successful, respected leader.

   The author is convinced that the more a leader uses MRT, the easier and more effective the application of structure becomes. When a subordinate is receiving the right rewards, he or she will accept structure

CASE 12: COMPATIBILITY

because structure protects and continues the reward system. Both parties come out ahead. Of course, it is possible to be a compassionate leader in the modern military establishment.

CASE 13: VIEWPOINT

Both viewpoints deserve support. Mr. Bello makes a strong point when he states there is a time lag between when decisions are made and when they are judged good or bad. Unfortunately, because of this we seldom have knowledge of the decision-making track records of our leaders. Ms. James is also right when she states that a poor decision can come home to haunt a leader. This is always a risk, as every long-term leader has discovered. None of the leaders I interviewed thought the Formula overstated the importance of decision making; some, however, suggested that it be given more weight among the basic foundations. The phrase "The buck stops here" emerged in many conversations, an indication that leaders know they live with the pressure of making decisions. This responsibility may dissuade many people from assuming leadership roles.

CASE 14: DECISION

The author strongly supports the two trustees who believe it is most difficult to verify the decision-making ability of an applicant. As for submitting their records in advance, it is naive to think that they would not construct them to make themselves look good. The best way to gain insight into the decision-making capabilities of an applicant is to ask the following questions during the interview stage: "How important is decision making to leadership?" "Do you feel you are a good decision maker? Why?" "Do you have a tested process you follow in making decisions? What is it?" Answers to these questions should be most revealing and provide the interview board with the data it needs on this vital subject. Is the board placing too much emphasis on decision making? Absolutely not! The destiny of any organization is determined more by the quality of decisions than by any other factor.

CASE 15: SUB-MISSIONS

It would be ideal if the leader of a sizable organization could create and communicate an overriding purpose (mission) so powerful and involving that it would preclude the need for separate departmental missions. In such a situation, sub-missions might even do more harm than good. It might be a mistake, however, to say that smaller groups within the framework of a large organization should not have the opportunity to develop missions of their own. A primary purpose of a mission is to make a group more cohesive, provide direction, and furnish an identity. If smaller organizations like churches, ball teams, and volunteer groups can benefit from the creation of a mission as opposed to a goal, then it makes sense that branches, divisions, or departments within a large organization could also benefit. The author supports both views but leans in the direction of the professor, because it would be a mistake to discourage departmental managers from giving serious thought to a mission for their employees. What if the top leader of the organization has failed to come up with a motivating mission?

Although Mrs. Loring states she believes in participatory management, in this case her plan appears to be too heavy-handed to work. Leaders at all levels must want to come up with missions. When it becomes a requirement, it can become a perfunctory assignment with no meaning. It is the position of the author that missions should come from *inside* leaders, not outside. Missions *and* leaders must reflect the needs (rewards) of the members of the group and provide vision beyond current goals. In some departments, this may not be possible. Therefore, to require each department manager to come up with a slogan may do more damage than good. The plan might work, however, on a volunteer basis. At least a few departments might create missions that would be meaningful. It is just not realistic to think this could happen in all departments.

CASE 16: INVOLVEMENT

Although charisma can be an irreplaceable asset to a leader, especially in the political arena, it is not essential. A leader with charisma may communicate a positive force more easily, but a positive force can be established without it, as Rebecca states. In fact, some leaders lean so heavily on charisma that they ignore the other, more powerful elements necessary to establish a positive force. It would be difficult, perhaps impossible, to build a case that a positive attitude is a charismatic characteristic. Charisma is a mix of traits that communicates a certain magic to followers; attitude is the way the leader looks at things mentally. Group members respond enthusiastically to any leader who has a positive attitude, perhaps because they want to believe in their leaders and the direction they are being asked to take. A charismatic leader may provide excitement, but a positive leader provides hope. The combination of both is, of course, ideal.

CASE 17: CHARISMA

It would appear that Ms. Grey overestimates the importance of communications in transmitting J. B.'s positive force; on the other hand, Mr. Fisher may be underestimating the role of public relations. It is impossible to say how far the positive force of a leader can be transmitted personally and when the communication network should take over. The leader of a small group (Boy Scout leader) may not need any help from a formal communication system, but the President of the United States needs all the help available. The balance required between the two is probably determined by the size of the group and the number of members who may be some

CASE 18: COMMUNICATIONS

distance away. A utility with 9000 employees certainly needs a two-level, two-way communication network if the positive force of the leader is to reach everyone. By the same token, Ms. Grey is lucky to have a leader who does so much on his own.

**CASE 19:
EMPHASIS**

The author defends Aaron and his balanced strategy. Only through the integration of all foundations into one's style will full benefits occur. Overemphasis of one or more foundations can be dangerous because of the interrelationships between all. Taking this stand, however, does not mean that Rose will not benefit. It is possible (not covered in the case) that Rose is already excellent at MRT and her decision-making capabilities are high. In this case she is filling in weak spots, and her strategy will work. For most people, however, Aaron's strategy is best.

**CASE 20:
PREDICTION**

Weaving the Formula into one's style requires follow-through if success is to be achieved, so it would appear that Jill has a decided edge over Janice. People who make a big thing about behavioral changes often put on a good show, but no permanent change takes place. This is a possibility with Janice. Jill's low-key approach may also offer benefits from a human relations point of view. Her coworkers may not sense ahead of time that she is becoming a strong leader, so no negative or jealous waves from others may develop. The danger of "coming on too strong" is always present when behavioral changes are made. Putting more leadership into your style should be a slow, sound, and permanent process for the best results.

CHAPTER 1

1. T
2. T
3. T
4. T (This is highly recommended.)
5. T
6. F (A primary advantage of the Formula in Chapter 3 is that it can be used at all management levels.)
7. T
8. T (They would, however, be better leaders if they became better managers.)
9. T
10. F (It's the balance that counts.)

CHAPTER 2

1. T
2. T
3. F (Usually the other way around.)
4. F
5. F
6. F
7. T
8. F
9. T
10. T

CHAPTER 3

1. F (Psychologists have been unable to do this.)
2. F (Just the opposite. The higher you get, the *more* opportunities there are—because so many potential leaders have fallen by the wayside.)
3. F (Coaches, ministers, military officers, and other leaders have also been involved.)
4. T (Most have used others as models, but have done it pretty much on their own.)
5. T (The success of one is sometimes dependent on the use of another.)
6. T (This is controversial, but the author sticks with the basic premise.)
7. F (It is a vital part, woven into all foundations.)
8. F (With their compassion for people, they might find some parts easier.)
9. T

10. T   (It is the contention of the author that the essence of leadership cannot be adequately explained in a single sentence or paragraph.)

CHAPTER 4

1. T
2. F   (Both are important.)
3. F
4. T
5. T
6. F   (The scale is only one signal. Besides, many successful leaders overcome early communication handicaps.)
7. T
8. F
9. T
10. T

CHAPTER 5

1. T
2. T   (This is a premise of the theory.)
3. T
4. F   (They provide too few, and often the wrong ones.)
5. T   (This is a primary advantage of MRT.)
6. F   (The ultimate franchise to lead comes from followers.)
7. T
8. T
9. F   (Like anything else, it requires commitment and practice.)
10. T

CHAPTER 6

1. T   (This a very strong recommendation for MRT.)
2. T   (Too much structure or discipline without MRT can lower productivity instead of increasing it.)
3. F   (Role power comes from the position one occupies.)
4. F   (They normally expand personality power and diminish role power.)
5. F   (They often do not balance their knowledge power with their role and personality power.)
6. T
7. T
8. F   (It is estimated that only about 10 percent of successful leaders have recognizable charisma.)

9. F (Leaders make greater use of personality power.)
10. T (Followers will recognize this sooner than most other efforts.)

CHAPTER 7

1. T
2. F
3. F
4. F (A prescribed, logical pattern is recommended, however.)
5. T
6. T
7. F (May produce a better decision, seldom faster.)
8. T
9. F
10. F (Lack of time forces many so-called gut decisions.)

CHAPTER 8

1. F (A mission is at a higher level, less practical, etc.)
2. F (A mission helps create and sustain a positive force.)
3. T
4. T
5. T
6. F
7. F (Articulation is usually the most difficult.)
8. F
9. F
10. T

CHAPTER 9

1. T
2. T
3. T (Some more than others, but some capacity is there.)
4. T
5. F (A positive force cannot be created without them.)
6. F (A two-way communications network is needed.)
7. T
8. T
9. T
10. T

CHAPTER 10

1. F (It is a do-it-yourself project.)
2. F

3. F   (MRT, e.g., can be applied in all human relationships.)
4. F
5. F
6. T
7. T
8. T   (This is especially true when it comes to applying more struc-
        ture without MRT.)
9. T
10. T

Leadership Effectiveness Scale

INSTRUCTIONS

This survey describes thirty-six (36) practices that are commonly demonstrated by acknowledged leaders. Please read each statement carefully. Then decide the extent to which each practice is characteristic of the person being rated. Then indicate your decision by circling the appropriate code to the right of each practice.

The person being rated:	Strongly Agree	Somewhat Agree	Somewhat Disagree	Strongly Disagree
1. Keeps followers fully informed.	SA	SWA	SWD	SD
2. Expresses thoughts clearly and forcefully.	SA	SWA	SWD	SD
3. Speaks well from a platform.	SA	SWA	SWD	SD
4. Is a good listener.	SA	SWA	SWD	SD
5. Attracts others to want to hear what he/she has to say.	SA	SWA	SWD	SD
6. Communicates a sense of "being in charge."	SA	SWA	SWD	SD
7. Converts employees into followers.	SA	SWA	SWD	SD
8. Demonstrates compassion for others.	SA	SWA	SWD	SD
9. Provides rewards that are important to followers.	SA	SWA	SWD	SD
10. Strives to win by allowing followers to also win.	SA	SWA	SWD	SD
11. Attracts others to want to join his/her group.	SA	SWA	SWD	SD
12. Has the full backing of all those who work under him/her.	SA	SWA	SWD	SD
13. Provides enough structure to create a cohesive feeling among his/her subordinates.	SA	SWA	SWD	SD
14. Establishes an authority line that is clear, consistent and appropriate for the situation.	SA	SWA	SWD	SD
15. Utilizes role, personality, and knowledge power in a balanced, effective manner.	SA	SWA	SWD	SD
16. Gets tough when necessary.	SA	SWA	SWD	SD

The person being rated:	Strongly Agree	Somewhat Agree	Somewhat Disagree	Strongly Disagree
17. Is respected by subordinates when authority is used.	SA	SWA	SWD	SD
18. Uses the power that he/she has with firmness but also with sensitivity.	SA	SWA	SWD	SD
19. Consults with others before making important decisions.	SA	SWA	SWD	SD
20. Has a strong track record for making solid decisions.	SA	SWA	SWD	SD
21. Follows a logical pattern in making decisions.	SA	SWA	SWD	SD
22. Stages and communicates decisions with pride and decisiveness.	SA	SWA	SWD	SD
23. Is able to admit mistakes when he/she makes them.	SA	SWA	SWD	SD
24. Faces up to and makes hard decisions.	SA	SWA	SWD	SD
25. Always maintains an upbeat attitude.	SA	SWA	SWD	SD
26. Articulates an inspiring mission to all employees/followers.	SA	SWA	SWD	SD
27. Generates a feeling of pride and higher productivity in followers.	SA	SWA	SWD	SD
28. Ties short-term work goals to inspirational missions.	SA	SWA	SWD	SD
29. Makes work more enjoyable.	SA	SWA	SWD	SD
30. Shares both large and small victories with followers.	SA	SWA	SWD	SD
31. Gets others caught up in his/her positive force.	SA	SWA	SWD	SD
32. Creates an active tempo that others want to emulate.	SA	SWA	SWD	SD
33. Reflects a positive attitude during difficult or tough times.	SA	SWA	SWD	SD
34. Is highly energetic and refuses to be "desk bound".	SA	SWA	SWD	SD

The person being rated:	Strongly Agree	Somewhat Agree	Somewhat Disagree	Strongly Disagree
35. Inspires others to be all they can be.	SA	SWA	SWD	SD
36. If she or he resigned, others would want to follow.	SA	SWA	SWD	SD

SCORING INSTRUCTIONS

Determine the point value for your response to each item and enter it in the score column. Total the scores for all six items in each category to obtain the CATEGORY SCORE. Then enter the scores for each category in the SCORE column of the summary section. Total the category scores to obtain the LEADERSHIP EFFECTIVENESS SCORE.

Leader as STAR COMMUNICATOR

Item:	SA	SWA	SWD	SD	Score
1.	4	3	2	1	_____
2.	4	3	2	1	_____
3.	4	3	2	1	_____
4.	4	3	2	1	_____
5.	4	3	2	1	_____
6.	4	3	2	1	_____

Category Score = _____

Leader as CREATOR OF FOLLOWERS

Item:	SA	SWA	SWD	SD	Score
7.	4	3	2	1	_____
8.	4	3	2	1	_____
9.	4	3	2	1	_____
10.	4	3	2	1	_____
11.	4	3	2	1	_____
12.	4	3	2	1	_____

Category Score = _____

Leader as POWER FIGURE

Item:	SA	SWA	SWD	SD	Score
13.	4	3	2	1	_____
14.	4	3	2	1	_____
15.	4	3	2	1	_____
16.	4	3	2	1	_____
17.	4	3	2	1	_____
18.	4	3	2	1	_____

Category Score = _____

Leader as DECISION MAKER

Item:	SA	SWA	SWD	SD	Score
19.	4	3	2	1	_____
20.	4	3	2	1	_____
21.	4	3	2	1	_____
22.	4	3	2	1	_____
23.	4	3	2	1	_____
24.	4	3	2	1	_____

Category Score = _____

Leader as a VISIONARY

Item:	SA	SWA	SWD	SD	Score
25.	4	3	2	1	_____
26.	4	3	2	1	_____
27.	4	3	2	1	_____
28.	4	3	2	1	_____
29.	4	3	2	1	_____
30.	4	3	2	1	_____
Category Score =					_____

Leader as POSITIVE FORCE

Item:	SA	SWA	SWD	SD	Score
31.	4	3	2	1	_____
32.	4	3	2	1	_____
33.	4	3	2	1	_____
34.	4	3	2	1	_____
35.	4	3	2	1	_____
36.	4	3	2	1	_____
Category Score =					_____

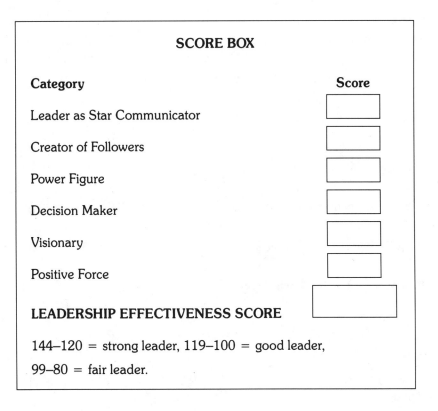

SCORE BOX

Category	Score
Leader as Star Communicator	
Creator of Followers	
Power Figure	
Decision Maker	
Visionary	
Positive Force	
LEADERSHIP EFFECTIVENESS SCORE	

144–120 = strong leader, 119–100 = good leader,
99–80 = fair leader.

Leadership Effectiveness Scale

INSTRUCTIONS

This survey describes thirty-six (36) practices that are commonly demonstrated by acknowledged leaders. Please read each statement carefully. Then decide the extent to which each practice is characteristic of the person being rated. Then indicate your decision by circling the appropriate code to the right of each practice.

The person being rated:	Strongly Agree	Somewhat Agree	Somewhat Disagree	Strongly Disagree
1. Keeps followers fully informed.	SA	SWA	SWD	SD
2. Expresses thoughts clearly and forcefully.	SA	SWA	SWD	SD
3. Speaks well from a platform.	SA	SWA	SWD	SD
4. Is a good listener.	SA	SWA	SWD	SD
5. Attracts others to want to hear what he/she has to say.	SA	SWA	SWD	SD
6. Communicates a sense of "being in charge."	SA	SWA	SWD	SD
7. Converts employees into followers.	SA	SWA	SWD	SD
8. Demonstrates compassion for others.	SA	SWA	SWD	SD
9. Provides rewards that are important to followers.	SA	SWA	SWD	SD
10. Strives to win by allowing followers to also win.	SA	SWA	SWD	SD
11. Attracts others to want to join his/her group.	SA	SWA	SWD	SD
12. Has the full backing of all those who work under him/her.	SA	SWA	SWD	SD
13. Provides enough structure to create a cohesive feeling among his/her subordinates.	SA	SWA	SWD	SD
14. Establishes an authority line that is clear, consistent and appropriate for the situation.	SA	SWA	SWD	SD
15. Utilizes role, personality, and knowledge power in a balanced, effective manner.	SA	SWA	SWD	SD
16. Gets tough when necessary.	SA	SWA	SWD	SD

The person being rated:	Strongly Agree	Somewhat Agree	Somewhat Disagree	Strongly Disagree
17. Is respected by subordinates when authority is used.	SA	SWA	SWD	SD
18. Uses the power that he/she has with firmness but also with sensitivity.	SA	SWA	SWD	SD
19. Consults with others before making important decisions.	SA	SWA	SWD	SD
20. Has a strong track record for making solid decisions.	SA	SWA	SWD	SD
21. Follows a logical pattern in making decisions.	SA	SWA	SWD	SD
22. Stages and communicates decisions with pride and decisiveness.	SA	SWA	SWD	SD
23. Is able to admit mistakes when he/she makes them.	SA	SWA	SWD	SD
24. Faces up to and makes hard decisions.	SA	SWA	SWD	SD
25. Always maintains an upbeat attitude.	SA	SWA	SWD	SD
26. Articulates an inspiring mission to all employees/followers.	SA	SWA	SWD	SD
27. Generates a feeling of pride and higher productivity in followers.	SA	SWA	SWD	SD
28. Ties short-term work goals to inspirational missions.	SA	SWA	SWD	SD
29. Makes work more enjoyable.	SA	SWA	SWD	SD
30. Shares both large and small victories with followers.	SA	SWA	SWD	SD
31. Gets others caught up in his/her positive force.	SA	SWA	SWD	SD
32. Creates an active tempo that others want to emulate.	SA	SWA	SWD	SD
33. Reflects a positive attitude during difficult or tough times.	SA	SWA	SWD	SD
34. Is highly energetic and refuses to be "desk bound".	SA	SWA	SWD	SD

The person being rated:	Strongly Agree	Somewhat Agree	Somewhat Disagree	Strongly Disagree
35. Inspires others to be all they can be.	SA	SWA	SWD	SD
36. If she or he resigned, others would want to follow.	SA	SWA	SWD	SD

SCORING INSTRUCTIONS

Determine the point value for your response to each item and enter it in the score column. Total the scores for all six items in each category to obtain the CATEGORY SCORE. Then enter the scores for each category in the SCORE column of the summary section. Total the category scores to obtain the LEADERSHIP EFFECTIVENESS SCORE.

Leader as STAR COMMUNICATOR

Item:	SA	SWA	SWD	SD	Score
1.	4	3	2	1	_____
2.	4	3	2	1	_____
3.	4	3	2	1	_____
4.	4	3	2	1	_____
5.	4	3	2	1	_____
6.	4	3	2	1	_____
Category Score =					_____

Leader as CREATOR OF FOLLOWERS

Item:	SA	SWA	SWD	SD	Score
7.	4	3	2	1	_____
8.	4	3	2	1	_____
9.	4	3	2	1	_____
10.	4	3	2	1	_____
11.	4	3	2	1	_____
12.	4	3	2	1	_____
Category Score =					_____

Leader as POWER FIGURE

Item:	SA	SWA	SWD	SD	Score
13.	4	3	2	1	_____
14.	4	3	2	1	_____
15.	4	3	2	1	_____
16.	4	3	2	1	_____
17.	4	3	2	1	_____
18.	4	3	2	1	_____
Category Score =					_____

Leader as DECISION MAKER

Item:	SA	SWA	SWD	SD	Score
19.	4	3	2	1	_____
20.	4	3	2	1	_____
21.	4	3	2	1	_____
22.	4	3	2	1	_____
23.	4	3	2	1	_____
24.	4	3	2	1	_____
Category Score =					_____

Leader as a VISIONARY

Item:	SA	SWA	SWD	SD	Score
25.	4	3	2	1	_____
26.	4	3	2	1	_____
27.	4	3	2	1	_____
28.	4	3	2	1	_____
29.	4	3	2	1	_____
30.	4	3	2	1	_____
Category Score =					_____

Leader as POSITIVE FORCE

Item:	SA	SWA	SWD	SD	Score
31.	4	3	2	1	_____
32.	4	3	2	1	_____
33.	4	3	2	1	_____
34.	4	3	2	1	_____
35.	4	3	2	1	_____
36.	4	3	2	1	_____
Category Score =					_____

SCORE BOX

Category	Score
Leader as Star Communicator	☐
Creator of Followers	☐
Power Figure	☐
Decision Maker	☐
Visionary	☐
Positive Force	☐

LEADERSHIP EFFECTIVENESS SCORE ☐

144–120 = strong leader, 119–100 = good leader,
99–80 = fair leader.

Index